Love, Mom

KATHY VIKRE

BALBOA.PRESS
A DIVISION OF HAY HOUSE

Balboa Press books may be ordered through booksellers or by contacting:

Balboa Press
A Division of Hay House
1663 Liberty Drive
Bloomington, IN 47403
www.balboapress.com
844-682-1282

Because of the dynamic nature of the Internet, any web addresses or
links contained in this book may have changed since publication and
may no longer be valid. The views expressed in this work are solely those
of the author and do not necessarily reflect the views of the publisher,
and the publisher hereby disclaims any responsibility for them.

The author of this book does not dispense medical advice or prescribe the use
of any technique as a form of treatment for physical, emotional, or medical
problems without the advice of a physician, either directly or indirectly. The
intent of the author is only to offer information of a general nature to help you
in your quest for emotional and spiritual well-being. In the event you use any
of the information in this book for yourself, which is your constitutional right,
the author and the publisher assume no responsibility for your actions.

Print information available on the last page.

ISBN: 978-1-9822-5452-0 (sc)
ISBN: 978-1-9822-5454-4 (hc)
ISBN: 978-1-9822-5453-7 (e)

Library of Congress Control Number: 2020916911

Balboa Press rev. date: 09/22/2020

The death of a mother is the first sorrow wept without her.

—Abdulai Mansaray

Contents

Acknowledgments

I offer much appreciation to the following people for their support:

Colin Broderick, your writing workshops taught me how to pull a book together from the mountain of letters I had accumulated. I appreciate your patience with my novice writing.

Rae Broderick, your wellness coaching put my head in the right place.

Janitt Dott, your advice on this book when I had next to nothing on paper helped me get started.

Christina Houghtaling, your generous sharing of the letters my mother wrote to your mother added depth to my knowledge of my mother.

Eric and Sue Houghtaling, your memories of visits to Mom's house and the seashore touched me.

Jerry Houghtaling, your memories of Mom, your birth, and your childhood inspired me. What a sharp memory you have!

Kara Kilmer, your essay on my mother, "The Fashionable Dodo," gave me insights.

Kevin McCann, your editing my book and helping me to find a clear vision for it were game changing. I can't thank you enough for pointing me in the right direction.

Jody McGrath, your painting of my mother captures her beautiful and colorful spirit. My sincere thanks for this wondrous gift.

Geraldine Medas, my little sister, your memories filled in the gaps and helped make the book complete. It is as much yours as it is mine.

The sharp editorial team at Balboa Press, you found manuscript errors I didn't know existed and gave me valuable assistance with your comments.

Introduction

Almost everyone likes to receive letters in the mail, especially news from home. Thanks to my mother's steadfastness in letter writing, I got news from home once a week for about forty years. The bills, ads, and junk mail that also turned up in the mailbox have long been discarded and forgotten, but I saved every letter Mom wrote.

She began each handwritten letter with "Dear Kath" and ended each with "Love, Mom." Along with news from home, I got insights into her personality and sense of humor. I knew what she was thinking about, both the big things happening in her life and the small things. I found out what meals she had prepared, books she had read, movies she'd seen, and concerts she had attended. The letters showed what she was made of: Catholic beliefs, compassion, charity, and boundless energy. The letters were a treasure, a link to her life and times. They provided both a lifeline to me at a low point in my life and a happy ending to my story.

For a long time, I thought Mom's letters deserved to be shared. She was an interesting person who spoke her mind. Her letters reflected the times she lived in and her good old-fashioned values. Her life wasn't big, but it was full of common sense, tolerated no nonsense, and was well documented.

I wanted to write a book based on Mom's letters but wondered if I had the skills. Although I had published a handful of technical papers and wrote (what I considered) amusing Facebook posts, I had never written a book. I wondered if I could tell a story that people would want to read.

My technical writing skills had been sharpened by an especially good boss I had in the early 1980s. He edited my technical reports in red ink. At first, they were returned to me covered in red edit marks, but eventually, as I learned the elements of proper composition, my reports were clean. I knew I could write with grammatical correctness.

But to write a book requires an ability to tell an interesting story, to have well-developed characters and a good flow. Luckily, I found a writer who liked my story and wanted to work with me. We spent days putting together a structure, chapter headings, and an outline for what was going to be written in each chapter. He gave me a couple of simple rules: "Be honest" and "Don't be afraid of a chapter; just structure it, and a flow will come." So out of respect for my mother and a belief that her letters should be shared, this retired grandmother from the American Midwest decided to write that book.

This book is Mom's story and mine—our times and places, how our family survived hard times, and how I found peace after she died. Since everyone has a mother, perhaps this book will resonate with you.

In this book, you will find excerpts from Mom's letters interspersed with my text. The wording is unchanged from her handwritten letters. Mom was a natural writer. She wrote what she thought. Consider her writing about this warm memory:

> It was early Christmas morning during the depression years. I was old enough to realize what a hard time my parents had making ends meet, but young enough to hope that Santa would come.

I lay in my bed wondering and hoping, and finally edged out of it. I went into the living room. There was a beautiful doll and carriage! Many years have passed since that Christmas long ago, but because of the love and self-sacrifice on the part of my wonderful parents, I had a Christmas that I will never forget.

This letter reveals that Mom grew up during the Depression years and that she understood her family's poor economic situation. With the optimism of youth, she hoped for Christmas gifts that her parents were unlikely to be able to afford. But a miracle happened: she went into the living room to find a beautiful doll and a carriage. Years later, she remembered the joy of receiving those gifts and wrote about it. The love of this family radiates across the decades, and in this letter, it is forever Christmas. The air is chilly, but the fireplace is warm. Bright lights dot the Christmas tree, and the scent of fresh fir fills the room. The little children are exploding with joy.

Mom's handwriting was as familiar to me as my own. Holding her letters was like holding her hand. They brought me close to her. Today the letters sparkle like points of light, stars shimmering in the night sky, leading me back to her memory. She wrote me well over a thousand letters—a thousand points of light.

CHAPTER 1

Mom's Letters: A Thousand Points of Light

I begin with my mother's death. I'm relaxing on a sunny Midwest afternoon in June 2009, the day before the summer solstice. Nothing about the day is special, and I have no forewarnings. Miles away from me, on the East Coast, my mother is busy dying.

Although I have a crippling fear of flying, my plane ticket is booked, and I will visit her in a week. Despite Mom's illness, I'm looking forward to this visit because my daughter is coming with me, and I will have company on the flights. We would have visited sooner, but my daughter had to wait until she could get time off from work.

I fully expect Mom to be alive when we visit. Unexpectedly, on this Saturday afternoon, the phone rings. It's my sister, Geraldine, who says, "Mom died."

I am shocked speechless. For a few minutes, I can't pull together any rational thoughts. All I can do is wail. I finally manage to say, "I knew she was dying, but I didn't know she was dying today." Although my sister is younger than I, she calms me down with sympathetic words. We talk briefly. Then I curl up in a ball and cry for hours. I wonder what life will be like without my mother and whether I will survive.

Mom had been admitted to a nursing home a month prior to her death. At the age of eighty-four, she had been diagnosed with a metastatic cancer, and she was treated with chemotherapy and radiation. Over time, she developed complications, was hospitalized, and then was transported to the nursing home at the age of eighty-eight.

Although she was dying, she was still full of life. Until she was hospitalized, we talked on the phone every day about all the usual things. We never talked about her disease or its prognosis. She called her handsome oncologist Dr. McDreamy after a character on *Grey's Anatomy*. One day he opened her shirt to listen to her heart only to discover she wasn't wearing a bra. She was always a private woman, but I guess when you're in your eighties and have a stage-four cancer, you throw caution to the wind. She laughed with him and later with me over the phone. Mom was still Mom.

I had last visited her for a week in April that year. In the deepest part of my mind, I knew that Mom was slipping away. She slept a lot, and I missed her usually delightful company. I loved talking with her. She was well versed in news of the day and news of the family. I valued her conversations and her insights. She hadn't completed high school, but her common sense and self-learning greatly overshadowed a lack of formal education.

My mother was the best cook I ever knew. Prior to her illness, she made delicious meals whenever I visited. Usually, I arrived to a full-course turkey dinner, one of my favorites. That week in April, I got by on fast food and pizza. Mom no longer had the stamina to cook. I offered to fix meals for her, but she wasn't hungry. She accepted only the occasional cup of Lipton's tea with no milk or sugar.

During that last visit, hospice workers encouraged Mom to

talk about her dying and last wishes—to get things unsaid out in the open. First, they asked my mother if she wanted to say anything to my sister and me. The two of us sat quietly in the living room, thinking about what Mom would say. Emotional topics were not her forte. Finally, Mom said sadly, "I wish I had been a better mother."

Then the hospice workers asked my sister and me if we wanted to say anything to Mom. My sister said, "Mom, you've been a great mother!"

I nodded in agreement, but I was mute. I wanted to tell her I loved her, but I was too shy. We were a family who didn't readily speak endearments or hug each other. I bit my tongue so I wouldn't say the most important words I'd ever wanted to say. The time had come for speaking up, but I let it slip away. I wondered if I would get another chance.

Alone with Mom, I asked her if she was afraid to die. She said she wasn't afraid, but she didn't want to suffer the pains of terminal cancer. That April, Mom cried when I said goodbye, as she always did when we parted company. We both feared that would be the last time we would see each other, but we didn't dare to say the words. I put on a brave face and said, "Don't worry, Mom. I'll see you again soon." I never did.

After hearing from my sister that our mom had died, I stumbled through the next few weeks at home. I managed to go to work every day but cried whenever I was alone. I was a heavy drinker at the time; still, I was careful not to overdo it. But the nights were so painful. I didn't care how much I drank. I missed my mom.

After a few weeks, I flew back to the East Coast to help handle Mom's affairs. There was no wake or service to attend. My sister had arranged to have Mom's body delivered to the Boston University Medical Center for research, as she had wished. Dad's body had undertaken the same trip years earlier, as he had wished. I helped sort her affairs and her belongings. I thought it was the last time I could do something for her. As it turned out, I had one more thing to do.

During that visit, I decided to stay at Mom's house, as usual. The first time I entered the house after she died, everything was surreal. Mom's things were still there, but she wasn't. There was nothing to distract me as I walked through the unnaturally still house full of my mother's belongings. I grief-walked through the rooms now empty of her. The first night, I slept in my father's bed. I couldn't bring myself to sleep in Mom's bed or even look at it. It was the only bed she had ever had, and it was still hers.

When I woke up the next day, there was no familiar smell of bacon and eggs cooking. I heard no radio playing in the kitchen, no reassuring sound of life. The house was broken like my heart. Only my sobs cut the silence. With dread, I got up and began assessing what needed to be done.

All her things were exactly as she had left them before her hospitalization. As usual, the house was clean. Despite being terminally ill, tiny, fragile, wrinkled, silver-haired, and sick, Mom had managed to do her spring cleaning a few months before she died. She always believed that cleanliness was next to godliness. Her cleaning tools were old and heavy. I can still see her struggling to move the heavy vacuum cleaner up and down the stairs. But she always persevered with whatever was important to her.

My sister and I sorted her clothes. They looked so small and tired hanging in the closet, like doll clothes. We asked her close neighbor if she wanted anything. She took several outfits. She was as desperate to hold on to memories as we were.

While I was cleaning the refrigerator, seeing her food, it hit me that she would never be coming home. I viewed the half-used bottle of ketchup, open carton of orange juice, and jar of leftover olives as tragic reminders that my mother's life had ended. I saw the mug that had held her last cup of tea.

Mom had set up a trust so that my sister and I co-owned all her possessions, including the house and car. She never wanted to cause work for anyone, even after her death. All her papers were in order in a small pile on the desk. After taking care of what little banking and insurance business needed to be done, I packed my bags for the last time in Mom's house and flew back to the Midwest, where I lived. My sister went on to sell the house and car. Mom would have been surprised to know that the house was sold to her dentist's receptionist.

Later that summer, while her body was at Boston University for medical research, my sister wrote the following letter to Mom's caretaker so he and his students could get to know her humanity while studying her anatomy.

Dear Mr. B,

I wanted to share some information and history with you and your students. My mother was the oldest of four children, raised during the Great Depression, born of a German/Dutch father and Polish mother. She married my father in 1944, a Norwegian fishing captain. She raised two daughters and worked in a retail department store until her retirement. She enjoyed traveling and kept her home and yard impeccably clean; she was religious and attended church weekly or more.

She walked more than two miles a day until, in her early 80's, she suffered a blackout and fell during a walk, after which a cardiologist implanted a pacemaker. In 2006 she was diagnosed with cancer and had surgery and chemotherapy. The chemo irritated a peptic ulcer. In late 2008 she was hospitalized after a neighbor found her unconscious from blood loss due to the ulcer.

She suffered in silence and never gave in to depression. She managed to live alone in her home with little or no assistance until April 2009, when she was hospitalized for chemotherapy side-effects. She was then transferred to a nursing home. Her sense of humor and stamina never faded, right up until the disease caused her death on June 20.

I know you have seen only her body during these months. I wanted to share with you the person who she was, a loving daughter, sister, mother, grandmother, great-grandmother, and friend to many. Even though she was a small woman, she was the strongest person I have known.

Sincerely,
Gerrie, her younger daughter

Eventually, Boston University completed its research, cremated Mom's body, and sent her ashes to my sister.

I had already retired from my long-term job and lived by myself, as my second husband had died. It was a lonely life. I was clinically depressed and chronically anxious. I wasn't a socializer; I had a few acquaintances but no close friends other than my two daughters. I'd left most of my friends at the job when I retired. Although some of us tried to stay in touch, the relationships just weren't the same, and we drifted apart. For emotional comfort, I had my four cats and two rabbits to hug. I enjoyed spending time with my grandchildren, reading books, and watching movies. I built family trees and did a lot of reminiscing, but I wasn't looking forward to the future. I was stuck in place, mourning my losses. I had no mother, and I was miserable.

When I wrote this book, Mom had been gone for ten years,

and I lived in an Arts and Crafts bungalow with a big yard. Like Mom, I felt peaceful surrounded by nature. She and I both loved gardening and being outdoors.

I enjoy my house, which has a yard big enough to be the small park I made it into. It has evergreen trees across the back fence to provide privacy, including various pines and firs and my favorite, blue spruce. In addition, the yard is peppered with hardwood trees. A large old sycamore grows outside the sunroom. The leaves of a silver maple canopy the deck. The buckeye tree is a favorite of local kids, who like to gather the nuts when they fall. Each year, I do landscaping. I now have brick walls and paved garden paths; rock gardens; and lots of perennials, such as daylilies and coneflowers, for color. I use lighting accents from a line called Kensington Park. To me, they evoke Victorian England at twilight. The lighting is soft, and I can imagine nannies walking prams and children climbing a statue of Peter Pan.

Although the house was built in 1926, previous owners renovated the kitchen and bathrooms. I added the sunroom to bring in light and give views of outside. My house has old-age charm and modern conveniences, oak floors, and a hardwood staircase to the second-story bedrooms. I am comfortable in it.

I don't really need all the land I live on, but I would miss having a yard big enough to stroll through. I often walk past the heirloom roses, the lilacs, the rock gardens, and, finally, the pine trees. The yard is especially enchanting in the early morning, when dew covers the grass. That is when I like to sit on the deck, drink coffee, and, like Henry David Thoreau living on his beloved Walden Pond, appreciate my own sanctuary away from the busy world. On summer evenings, I watch the fireflies light the night with their tiny lanterns. I remember my mother giving me a jar in which to collect them and then let them go.

One Christmas, my sister sent me a gift package. As I opened it and started taking out homemade cookies and colorfully wrapped presents, one object caught my attention. In a bottle with a decorative top were half of Mom's ashes. My sweet sister wanted to share them with me, as we had shared everything else that had been Mom's. Emotions washed over me as I realized that in a way, Mom had come home to me. I put the bottle holding Mom's ashes on a shelf in the den.

For decades, Mom had sent me a handwritten letter every week, which I read and then tossed into a cardboard box in an upstairs linen closet. I could never bear to throw away her letters, and many had accumulated—I guessed there were hundreds in that box. I had planned to do something with her letters, but ten years passed before I was able to face the daunting task. As William Shakespeare said, "The readiness is all." I was in my seventies and considering my own mortality. I had to do something soon or risk not doing it. No one lives forever.

I moved the box of letters downstairs to the den and glanced at the shelf that held Mom's ashes. I paused as I observed all that was left of my mother: her ashes and her words. I desperately needed to hear from her. I was a little girl looking for her mother, and I believed I would find her in her letters.

While I was growing up, we were a family of readers; we loved books and often shared our opinions and reading lists. Mom, Dad, my sister, and I always had a book going. Mom sometimes read two at a time, one upstairs and one downstairs. In addition to being a reader, Mom was a writer. She wrote letters to me, her sister, her nieces and nephews, sisters-in-law, and others. While her letters were casual in tone, she made sure they were grammatically correct. In fact, she encouraged me to correct her if I ever heard her use a word incorrectly. She expanded her vocabulary by learning new words, such as *obsequious, pejorative,* and *supercilious.* Although she wanted to learn new words, she kept her letters colloquial and didn't try to impress anyone with her new vocabulary. Here's what she said in one of her letters:

> I learned a new word this week. I'm reading a
> book and came across "desultory." I'm hoping I
> can use it someday if I remember it & the right
> occasion comes up.

Writing letters by hand takes time, and Mom gave it priority. She wrote to the same people at the same time of the week. My letters were written on Tuesday mornings. I watched Mom write some of her letters and saw how she put things aside to make room for her communications. I learned that you can always make time for what is important to you.

Mom wrote on any kind of stationery she could find that was inexpensive. Much of what she used was a gift from someone or another. If she had to buy paper, it was always from Job Lot. Mom put emphasis on what she had to say, not on what writing paper she used, and she wrote with ballpoint pens until they ran out of ink. Occasionally, the ink ran out in the middle of a letter, and a different pen was used to finish it. Being a child of the Great Depression, she was always conscientious about spending money wisely. The result of her decades of letter writing was a box filled with mixed-color papers of all sizes, shapes, and colors, in no order at all.

I was glad I had kept her letters. We had talked on the phone during the decades when the letters were being written, but there were no records of those calls. The words spoken on the phone had faded into the air, while those in the letters were still in the cardboard box to be read and treasured.

The box was about two feet square and almost filled to the top. Her letters were usually three pages long and folded twice, which kept most of the pages together. But as I looked into the box I saw chaos: some letters had come apart, individual pages were scattered throughout, and some were crumpled or torn. Forty years of letters had been tossed helter-skelter into this box. The task of bringing order to the chaos was daunting. I wondered how many complete letters I could reassemble.

First, I emptied the contents of the box onto the floor and sorted the letters by decade. My four cats had a field day during that time. They thought I was littering the floor for their amusement. They batted the letters out of my hands, stole them, and chased and chewed them. The path to Mom's words coursed through a tangle of kitties.

As the cats allowed me, I piled the four decades (1970s through 2000s) into whatever big containers I could find: a bookcase, a laundry basket, and so on. Then I bought twelve identical plastic bins, each the size of a small baby. I placed them on a folding table and labeled them by month, "Jan" to "Dec." A friend commented that the bins looked like a row of newborns in a hospital nursery.

Working within a decade, I pulled all the letters written in January and placed them in the "Jan" bin and so on until the decade pile had been transferred to the month bins. To reconstruct a particular year's worth of letters, I went through each month bin and pulled the letters written in that year. When I had processed one decade of letters, I emptied the bins and started over with the next decade. It was hard work, but I was capable of doing it and proud of what I was doing, bringing order to chaos. By the time I finished, I had found and assembled more than twelve hundred letters, each a point of light to help me find a way to my mom. Only a few letters were missing pages, and just a few pages were missing letters.

Next, I reread each letter and entered selected portions into a computer file. Once online, the excerpted letters could be searched. Without an online aid, they were as useful for finding information on a topic as they had been while scattered in the box. Emptying the boxes, rereading the letters, and getting the excerpts into a computer took about six months. It was a labor of love.

As I read them, the letters brought back many memories. It was as if Mom were still with me, and I found myself wanting to call her for more details on what she had written about.

Within the letters, I found the births of babies, the deaths of relatives, and Mom's thoughts about them. I found one story about my young mother writing letters to her three great-aunts in the 1930s. Since her grandmother didn't know how to write, her grandmother dictated the letters to her. My mom had been writing letters for almost eighty years!

As I read the letters, I was reminded of her relationship with Dad. She wrote,

> Your father had a fit because I was out so long. He forgets all the times he was out getting bombed while I was home.

> Your father almost got us killed just at the bottom of the hill. A car came at us from the right going really fast. There wasn't a stop sign but the other car seemed to think he had the right of way. I know he saw us & he was coming right at us. I screamed and then your father saw him. I was surprised that he did admit that he didn't see the other car.

While he lived, Dad was in every letter. So was my sister. It was clear how close she and Mom had been. My sister didn't have an easy life, and I was glad to see how my parents had helped her. Seeing things in writing gave me a broader perspective. I saw things now that I hadn't seen when I first read the letters. I was older and wiser, reading with hindsight.

It was especially hard to read about the illnesses that I knew ended in death; it was like being able to see the future and knowing that it was going to hurt when it came. At times, I was so emotionally caught up that I felt like stopping. But seeing Mom's handwriting and knowing her tenacity kept me going. If she could write those letters, then the least I could do was reread them. And I needed to find my mom. I had known her from my first breath, and she was gone from me.

My mother was a good person, and she had a story to tell. Writing a book based on her letters was the last thing I could do for her. It would be a book she would have been proud of and one I would be proud to give my children. To get ready to write, I shared and compared memories with my sister. I talked to my uncle Jerry, Mom's brother, and pored through old photographs. I took two writing workshops. Finally, I found a mentor who was willing to work closely with me. I was ready and began writing the book.

CHAPTER 2

My Mother the Star

My mom loved Hollywood. She loved the fun, magic, and glamour of it. Consequently, she loved going to movies, reading celebrity biographies and movie magazines, singing, and dancing. As a child, she dreamed of singing and playing the piano. When she was a young lady, she started calling herself Star and told the boys she dated that that was her name. She was always my shining star in the sky, helping me to find my way home. From my earliest years, she was the star of my life.

The lovely lady who was to become my mother was born in 1921 in a tiny yellow brick house on Hanratty Street in Kingston, New York. She was named Dorothy, meaning "gift of God." Her middle name was Catherine after her mother. Almost everyone called her Dot. Although she didn't know it, she was descended from the early Dutch settlers of New York City and from ancestors who'd lived in Prussia, Poland, Germany, and other Middle European areas.

Kingston is a city on the shores of the Hudson River, about ninety miles upriver from New York City. The house, built in 1870, was perched on the steep hill that was Hanratty Street, which had no flat sections. All the houses on Hanratty Street were on the hill, so the houses looked like stair steps going up and down.

Her parents, Kate and Bill Hotaling, were born in the last years of the nineteenth century. The surname is now spelled Houghtaling, but I prefer the older version because it's easier to read. Kate was called Nan by her grandchildren. Bill was called Pop. Kate was born in 1897, two years before Bill. The fact that she was older bothered her. In fact, she insisted that her birth date not be carved on her headstone. It wasn't.

My grandmother Nan was a sweet, gentle woman who loved babies and could always get them to stop crying. Consequently, she was given a lot of crying babies to hold. She would rock them back and forth in her comfortable, chubby arms and softly sing to them, and they would stop crying. She was a caring and affectionate person, and I loved her deeply. For a time, as a youngster, I thought I could handle my mother's death but not my grandmother's. She was a devout Catholic; all her actions reflected a deep and abiding love of God, family, and neighbor. She passed her faith along to her four children.

My grandfather Bill came from a long line of Hotalings, including soldiers in the Revolutionary War. His line can be traced to the original family immigrants, Jan Willem and Barbara Jans, who came to America from the Netherlands in 1661.

Bill lived to the age of sixty-five, when he died of a heart attack. His death was attributed to the so-called Hotaling curse, a family legend that males in the family died at the age of sixty-five from heart disease. In addition to the soldiers, Bill came from a long line of bad hearts. Mom mentions the bad hearts in her letters:

> I just got a phone call from my brother Billy. He's been in Boston for tests. He finally got results and his dizziness is heart-related. In time he may need another operation.

Billy had another heart attack & is in the hospital.

Cousin Paul died. Another Hotaling heart death.
He died picking tomatoes like *The Godfather.*

Pop cut an imposing figure. He was tall, quiet, sober, and strict. Mom said that none of her siblings dared to talk back to him. Growing up, I was also a little afraid of him. He loosened up, joked, and talked only after a beer or two. One Saturday night during my childhood, he showed up at my family's house in Massachusetts, two hundred miles from Kingston. At first, we were thrilled to see him—then we realized he was alone. Where was Nan? It seemed she and Pop had had an argument, and he had driven for nearly eight hours to get a breather. He insisted that my mother not call Nan to tell her where he was. That was unthinkable since my grandmother would be worried, so of course Mom called her. I can still hear her whispering into the phone, "Mom, he's here." My mother was respectful and obedient to both her parents, but she would never intentionally cause either of them to worry.

Mom was the oldest of four children. Dorothy, Tillie, and Billy were born between 1921 and 1925. The fourth, Jerry, came later. They were skinny kids with the same bowl haircut and the same brown Hotaling eyes. They were bright and fun-loving. The siblings never fought with one another. Mom recalled their relationship in a letter:

> I never remember Tillie, Billy or I fighting with each other. I was the oldest & Tillie & Billy shared their goodies with me. At Easter time I would eat my candy & then they shared theirs with me. I was selfish enough to do this. One Christmas Tillie & I got a doll & carriage, Billy got a small pool table. I can't remember where we

put it because the house was so small. Billy had a wooden scooter & he would go down the hill like a streak of lightning. He was the talk of the neighborhood, he was so fast.

As a child, Mom loved to sing and listen to the radio. She once sang a song on a local radio station ("A Tisket, a Tasket") and was proud of that accomplishment all her life. As an adult, she listened to the songs on *Your Hit Parade* and sang along with them. She sang when she did housework, and she sang as she gardened. She was always singing. No doubt she inherited her beautiful singing voice from her father, who often sang in local minstrel shows. He was a pitch-perfect baritone, and she was a spot-on soprano.

Every Saturday during the 1930s, the Hotaling kids cleaned the house. They washed the kitchen table and chairs, dusted, cleaned the windows, and aired the bedding. My mother ran errands. She often went grocery shopping for her mother at Abel's Market, a small mom-and-pop store just across the railroad tracks at the bottom of the street. Occasionally, she sampled the food before she got home. One time, she ate an entire box of cream cheese, which made her sick. She walked to Mike's, a local bar, to buy a growler of beer for her father. You could get the growler filled for twenty-five cents, and filling it for a child to bring home was no problem. She also walked to Nick's, a general store, to buy cigarettes for her father.

The kids bathed on Sunday morning in a steel tub that was carried into the warm kitchen from an unheated storeroom. The tub was filled slowly with pots of water that had been heated on the stove. Once filled, the tub was used by all the kids without a change of water. There was no privacy. To get the cleanest, hottest water and some degree of privacy, Mom took her bath first—at sunrise.

The siblings walked to school and to weekly Mass. The elementary school stood at the top of yet another steep hill. In the winter, the streets became so slippery with snow and ice that the janitor had to pull the kids up to the school on sleds. Catholic school life was strict. Students sat with their hands folded and backs erect. Once, my young mother looked out a window and was hit over the hand by a nun with a ruler. Mom was a good student and respected her teachers.

Throughout their lives, the Hotaling kids were close. I've never seen closer sisters than Mom and Tillie. As an adult, I loved to sit with them to hear them talk. Tillie always brought up things that had happened when they were kids. She told of the time they all had urinated into their empty steel bathtub and gotten whipped with a cat-o'-nine-tails for it. "We must have been really stupid," she had said, laughing. Tillie was a fun person with a great memory, and she laughed a lot. She was well versed in politics, especially New York politics, and since her husband worked at the post office, she knew many of the townspeople. She always amused us when she talked. She spoke with a mixture of knowledge, sarcasm, and wit. When my sister and I visited Kingston as children, Tillie often took us on the bus to go shopping uptown, and she usually bought us a small plaything. While waiting for the bus to take us home, we always got ice cream at the soda shop near the bus stop.

Tillie married, had two daughters, and became a widow. She was a widow for twelve years, and she loved living by herself. If a friend or neighbor called and she didn't want company, she would duck out of sight and not answer the door. She was a free spirit. She worried about nothing and couldn't have cared less about cleaning the house. Like the rest of her family, she had unshakeable faith in the Catholic church and lived almost in the backyard of the Polish church, her mother's church. I liked to go to that small church. Although I didn't understand a word of the Polish prayers and hymns, Father Joe, the monseigneur, was as friendly and welcoming as could be. Years later, during a memorial, the church remembered Tillie when she died.

Tillie and Mom spoke on the phone every Saturday. Later in life, Tillie had swollen legs and shortness of breath. One Saturday when Tillie was in her seventies, she had what seemed to be a bad cold. She was congested and coughing, and Mom was worried, but Tillie wasn't. On Monday, Mom received word that Tillie had died over the weekend while sitting in her favorite easy chair. Perhaps her heart had failed. Hearing the news was devastating to my mother. Tillie was her touchstone. They had grown up with the same memories, and they were best friends. Tillie was a happy person who could always make Mom laugh. When she died, she took part of my mother's heart with her. Mom mentions Karen, one of Tillie's two daughters, in the following letter about Tillie's death:

> My neighbor gave me a very pretty red rose bush in memory of Tillie. I called Karen last night to make sure she had a safe trip home. I figured Tillie wasn't here any more to worry about her. We're going to Kingston some week in July to clean out her house a little bit. I just watched *Regis & Kathie Lee* & there's so much I would like to talk to Tiilie about. Tillie has been waiting for a wedding that Regis is in & it took place over the weekend. They had the wedding video today & Tillie would have really enjoyed it.

Mom's brother Billy died at the age of sixty-five from heart disease, the Hotaling family curse. Once again, Mom was devastated; she so loved her family. I visited Billy's wife and children a few weeks after he died. Weeks earlier, the kids had made a video cassette of their parents' lives as a gift for their wedding anniversary. No one had had the heart to watch it since Billy died. We decided to shore each other up and watch as a group. We watched, and we cried as a group; the memories were beautiful and poignant. Years later, Mom wrote,

> Billy's birthday is coming up soon. Sometimes I wonder why he & Tillie went before me. Once you start thinking tho, you drive yourself crazy. I'm not as upbeat as I used to be. I got a letter from a funeral parlor asking me to make my final arrangements. How can you be upbeat when that's the kind of mail you get?

Mom's youngest brother, Gerard "Jerry" Hotaling, was born when my grandmother Kate was forty years old. In 1937, the pregnancy was considered high risk due to her age, as it would be today. When the doctor came to the house to deliver the baby, he brought along a little bag to carry the body in case the child didn't survive. Mom saw the doctor leave, looked for the bag, and heard her brother cry. He was named Gerard after the saint who takes care of expectant mothers. Mom reflects on his birth:

> Today is Jerry's birthday. I remember the day he was born. I sat in the window watching Pop pace up & down Hanratty St. I was almost 16 at the time. I was in my last year of high school & I had to leave to take care of him. It was during the depression & Nan went back to work.

At the age of sixteen, Mom became a full-time caretaker for her baby brother. Mom told me she didn't resent leaving high school in her senior year. Despite being a teenager, she didn't consider watching her brother to be a burden—it had to be done. That was the attitude of children who grew up in hard times, such as the Great Depression. Jerry always had a special place in Mom's heart, most likely because she was like a second mother to him as well as a devoted sister.

When Jerry started school, Mom got a job at the Manhattan Shirt Factory, worked eight hours a day, and brought home between fifteen and twenty dollars a week to help the family.

Her prettiness and fun-loving personality made her popular with the boys. She had lots of dates. One, Harry McCarthy, gave her his father's ruby ring, which, in time, she gave to me. When I wear his ring, I wonder what became of Harry. Many of the boys Mom knew went off to war and were killed. She never forgot her classmates who died in World War II. My mother lived through some of the hardest times the United States has faced: the Great Depression and World War II. Her generation, remembered and respected, is called the Greatest. During the war, material goods were scarce. Food was rationed, including staples, such as meat, sugar, and butter. It was a trying time for everyone. She once wrote this to me:

> Today is Pearl Harbor Day. It's funny I can remember it as if it were yesterday. The war was a very sad time in my life, I lost many schoolmates. They were killed in Germany and Japan in battle.

As my mother grew into a young adult, she went to the nightclubs for socializing. At the clubs in the 1940s, young men and women met, had a few drinks, danced, and got to know each other. I can see my five-foot-two-inch mother swing dancing to the music of Bing Crosby and Harry James, her dark brown curls bouncing up and down in time to the beat, her brown eyes sparkling, and her shiny red lips smiling the night away. She loved having a good time, and she laughed easily. She was a happy, bright spirit, a beautiful little songbird.

Near the end of the war, Mom and her girlfriends went to a popular Kingston nightspot called the Barn. A roving photographer took photos, and in one picture, Mom is sitting in a booth, wearing a short-sleeved striped sweater, and looks like a little doll.

At the Barn, she met a tall young man in uniform. He would have approached her timidly since he was shy in social situations. His name was Knut (pronounced "Cah-nute"), and he had immigrated to America from Norway at the age of ten. Handsome and fair, with hazel eyes and wire-rimmed glasses, he carried himself proudly like a general, but he was a sergeant in the Army Air Force and fixed airplanes. He spoke with an American accent, not the Norwegian she expected. In May 1944, about a month after meeting, Mom and Dad married in a Catholic ceremony at Stewart Air Field in Newburgh, New York, where he was stationed. They married in haste because he thought he was getting sent overseas. Mom took a Greyhound bus from Kingston to the wedding. Her young brother Jerry was not allowed to go and cried his heart out because he wanted to be with her.

In wedding photos, Mom is wearing a short white dress, white gloves, and a large corsage. She has a crown of flowers in her hair. Tillie, her maid of honor, wears a dress suit and corsage. Dad and his best man are in military uniform. Everyone is smiling. For their honeymoon, the newlyweds went to a Frank Sinatra concert in New York City.

I was born before the dust settled on their marriage, a mere ten months later. Like my mother, I began life in Kingston, New York. I was born at the Benedictine Hospital, a former tuberculosis sanitarium. In old photos, it looks like a haunted mansion. During labor, Mom was given a rope to tug on and a whiff of ether for the final push.

I was named Kathryn Marie after my grandmothers, Catherine and Marie. Mom chose to spell my first name as Kathryn because she liked the actress Kathryn Grayson.

During my first few months of life, I lived in that tiny house on Hanratty Street, where Mom learned to fret over me. When I had an early illness, the neighborhood mothers and grandmothers hovered over me and told my mother the likely causes of my impending demise. When the doctor came, he chased away the women and told my mother I had a cold. But even a cold was scary enough for Mom. She worried about my health until she died. If she was at all happy to die, one reason would have been that she didn't have to worry anymore. She always worried. She dreaded the birth of every child and grandchild. More family meant more people to worry about.

As an infant, I was fed every four hours, according to the book, whether I was hungry or not. Apparently, I was hungry most of the time, because I cried a lot. After the doctor told my mother to throw the book away, I was fed more often and was much more content.

When I was still a baby, we moved from Kingston to New Bedford, Massachusetts, a city on the Atlantic Ocean. New Bedford is a famous whaling and fishing port. It is an old city with cobblestone streets in its historic district and lots of textile mills, reflecting the rise of the textile industry after most of the whales had been killed.

For a while, we lived with Dad's parents, and Dad became a commercial fisherman; he fished for money, not sport. Mom wrote,

> When I first brought you to New Bedford it was in April & it was after the war. Coal was scarce & Nanny said she couldn't get any. I really don't think she tried too hard because it was a big job to go down to the furnace and make a fire. It was *so* cold in that house with no heat. I was afraid you would get sick. I called all the coal companies in New Bedford & I finally got somebody to deliver coke, which doesn't burn as long as coal. I was supposed to stay longer but I called Nan & she got Pop to drive down and bring us back to Kingston.

Nanny was my father's mother. My sister and I considered her an odd duck, but she taught us many valuable life lessons.

She was a tough, no-nonsense Norwegian woman who ran the home and farm in Norway while my grandfather worked and saved money in America. When summoned to join him, my grandmother sold the farm and the animals. She then made all the clothes for the long ocean voyage. My grandmother and my father crossed the Atlantic Ocean, were processed through Ellis Island, and reunited with my grandfather in Brooklyn, New York.

Eventually, Dad's parents moved to New Bedford, where they rented the first floor of a house built in 1850. It was a dark house; little sunlight came in through the small windows, and the furniture was made from dark wood, walnut and mahogany. Even as a youngster, I thought the house was quiet and austere like the Norwegians who lived there.

When I was a toddler, Mom tied a damp washcloth around my neck so I could be cleaned as soon as I got dirty. Apparently, dirt was full of germs that could make you sick. Mom's fear of germs might have initiated the hypochondria I later fell victim to. But as a youngster, I was physically active and fearless. Mom told me I was often covered from head to toe with bruises from my reckless behavior. I believe it—I once jumped off a garage roof.

When I was two, my baby sister was born, and we moved to an old gray-shingled house on Chestnut Street. It was located in a quiet residential area within walking distance of my grandparents, school, church, and the fishing boat piers. It was easy to see how Chestnut Street got its name. It was lined on both sides with mature chestnut trees, which dropped chestnuts and leaves to the ground. The green leaves changed to gold and orange in the fall. In my memory, Chestnut Street is emblazoned with these bright colors, and leaves cover every inch of the street and sidewalks.

I loved that old house, the house of my childhood. It had a wide, ornate wooden bannister between floors that my sister and

I used to slide down, lots of nooks and crannies, a hidden room where one of our cats had kittens, a butler's pantry, a root cellar, and even a widow's watch—a bay window on the second floor for spotting whaling ships. Although my sister and I each had a bedroom, we usually slept together. At bedtime, we were a bundle of kids, dolls, and stuffed animals. Next to the kitchen, we had a playroom where we kept all our toys—what luxury. The deep kitchen sink was made of slate. I cut my finger on it and still have the scar to remind me. The house had a living room and a parlor separated by French doors with glass panels. The parlor was empty except for a clunky old piano, which I played, and a table that Mom used for sorting laundry.

A lush row of lilies of the valley lined the backyard fence, and brightly colored hollyhocks climbed the chain links. No lily has ever had the sweet fragrance of those in my childhood yard. Father Murphy from St. Lawrence Church would occasionally stop by to chat with my mother over the fence. He made her feel welcome in the neighborhood when it was new to her. We went to Mass at his church, and later, Geraldine and I went to Holy Family School. As Mom watched from the window, I practiced gymnastics on the swing set in our backyard, and my sister and I played with tin soldiers in the sandbox. Once, we found a dead mouse in it. It was my first smell of death, something you never forget. The little gray mouse was dead and harmless, but it terrified my sister and me.

In those early years, Nanny invited our young family to dinner almost every Sunday. She set a fine table, using her best plates and sterling silver cutlery. She was a great cook and could make the toughest piece of meat taste delicious. I especially remember her rare and juicy roast beef; gelled fish pudding; and fish balls, which were mixtures of fish meat and spices shaped liked hamburger patties. The only thing I didn't like was her mutton. It's bad enough to eat a sheep, let alone a fatty old sheep! Her kitchen canisters had the names of the spices in Norwegian. At school, I would spell *sugar* as *sukker*, which puzzled the nuns who taught me. Whenever we were with Nanny, either at her place or at ours, when three o'clock came around in the afternoon, it was time for coffee and dessert.

Nanny liked to talk, and she was compelled to give advice; she liked to pass along newspaper clippings that she found important. She meant to help, but she drove my poor mother to distraction. She had opinions and instructions about everything. Long before serial killers arrived on the scene, she told my sister and me to be wary of strangers and to lock the car doors and close the car windows at all times. We didn't take her seriously, until society became as dangerous as my grandmother always thought it was.

Nanny was frugal almost to a fault. When my grandfather died, she converted all his trousers into skirts for herself. To save electricity, she toasted four pieces of bread in the morning, two for lunch and two for later in the day. One Christmas, she got irregular blankets for my sister and me. They were full of holes and not useable. We all had a good laugh, including Nanny. She never drove, and she walked great distances to go shopping and pay bills. I learned a lot about responsibility from her, and I picked up her habit of saving items from the newspaper.

As a child, I spent time in both New Bedford, where Mom and Dad lived, and Kingston, where Nan and Pop lived. For more than fifteen years, my sister and I spent every summer in Kingston with my mother.

The day after school let out for the summer, we headed to Kingston, and we didn't return until the day before school started. My father drove us, stayed for a couple of days, and then returned to New Bedford for a summer of commercial fishing. For years, we never saw Dad in the summer; we got so used to it that we hardly noted it. I remember Mom joking that Dad never changed the sheets while we were gone.

My sister and I were happy with the eight-hour car trip from New Bedford to Kingston, during which we would stop at Zip's Diner outside of Providence for coffee and pie and later at a dairy bar outside of Hartford for ice cream. We listened to Arthur Godfrey on the radio. My sister and I sang and played car games, guessing what color the next car would be or which state it would be from. Driving in upstate Connecticut was beautiful, especially in the snow, through those postcard-perfect towns, each of which seemed to have a white-steepled church in the center. Eventually, we reached Route 199, which took us to the car ferry that crossed the Hudson River into Kingston. When we arrived at Hanratty Street, our excitement overflowed. There were Nan and Pop!

One year, Mom decided to charter a small plane for our trip. It was my first flight. It was a Piper Cub, a really small plane, kind of like a truck with an extended cab and wings. Mom sat up front with the pilot, and my sister and I sat in the back, looking out the small windows. Mom fell asleep on the pilot's shoulder, and I got motion sick and threw up when the plane landed. On the way back, Pop drove us to New York City, and we flew back on a bigger plane, a propeller-driven Douglas DC-6.

In Kingston, we played Wiffle ball on the small side yard with my uncle Jerry and his friends. We rolled down the hill in the neighbor's backyard, loving the big dips in the hill and seeing who could get to the bottom first. We went swimming at Kingston Point Beach. Once, my sister and I thought we saw a body under the water, wedged against some rocks. We ran to Mom and told her. Mom agreed that it looked like a body. Upon close inspection, the body turned out to be a rubber baby doll. The creepy feeling I got from seeing the doll stayed with me, and deep water frightened me from then on.

The small backyard in Kingston sloped into a steep hill covered with grass that was often long and unkempt like prairie grass because it was hard to mow. Across the street from the bottom of the hill were a small cow barn and a few amiable cows in a corral. A ragman lived in a small house next to the barn. In the Great Depression era, rags were a commodity that were bought and sold. We bundled up any rags we could spare and sold them to the ragman for a few pennies. The ragman would then sell the rags and any other household goods he had accumulated.

On the front porch of the house, Pop sat on the green metal glider for hours, listening to the Yankees game on the radio, swatting flies, and letting their small corpses fall to the wooden floor. At times, I joined him, especially at night when it was too hot to sleep. From the porch, you could see a single streetlamp atop a tall wooden pole at the top of a steep dirt road that led to the Hasbrouck Park woods. That nighttime image stays with me. I have always appreciated the written word, so when I was forty years old, in 1985, I captured the memories in a poem:

> At midnight in August thirty years ago,
> On the porch of my grandparents' house
> In hot upstate New York,
> Slowly swinging on the glider and slapping mosquitoes,
> I notice that the neighbors can't sleep either,
> And they sit on their porches too.
>
> I focus on the streetlight
> At the top of the wooded hill
> Leading to the footpath that leads to the park.
> I think of wolves and werewolves.
> A dog lives on the park path which
> They say is half wolf, but he doesn't bother anyone.
>
> At night, the park shows movies on a cement screen,
> Which, in the morning, you can toss balls at.
> The movies are mostly scary ones of monsters,
> And the walk home past the wolf takes forever.

The whistle of a freight train pierces the midnight air
With a familiar hoot.

Kingston is at the foot of the Catskill Mountains, and thunderstorms can be severe. We knew when the air turned an eerie yellow that a storm was brewing. Nan always lit a prayer candle, but storms didn't scare my sister and me. Thunder was said to be the sound of Rip Van Winkle playing ninepins with Henry Hudson's crew. When the rain broke loose from the storm clouds, water would rush down Hanratty Street, and we'd put on our bathing suits and slide down the street with the water.

I have fond memories of those summers in Kingston, storms and swimming, walks to the park, lazy days on the porch glider, and sitting at the lunch table with a glass of homemade iced tea while reading comic books, such as *Little Lulu* and *Archie*. My uncle Jerry was an avid collector of comic books. He had an entire backyard shed full of them, and he always bought the newest editions.

But most of my childhood memories come from living in the house on Chestnut Street with Mom, Dad, Geraldine, and maybe a cat. That was where I went to school and church and the beach, made friends and boyfriends, and grew up.

Mom kept a fastidiously clean house and had a lifelong phobia of bugs. They didn't stand a chance in her home, as many of her letters proved:

> I spent most of the day trying to track down some ants. I had a few in the kitchen & I figured out they came in from the back hall. I took everything out of the closet & had your father fill in all of the cracks. I go crazy when I see a bug.
>
> I had a bad night last night. When I got into bed, I discovered a centipede in my room. For some

reason I seem to get 2 centipedes a yr. in my room & it's always in April. Since Apr. 1st I've been checking my room like a hawk. Last night I got a little careless & didn't check until I got in bed. When I saw it, I actually felt faint. Your father was asleep so I had to get the thing myself. I got it with a dust buster but I slept very little. Just writing about it now gives me chills.

Don't you think I found a centipede in my bedroom last night at midnight. I almost had a bird. It was on the ceiling. I got it with hair spray.

She also had an unusual fear of driving in the snow.

As I'm writing this all our power went off. This is the third time since the snowstorm that people have lost their power, but the first time for us. The weather has been terrible, wind, rain, snow. You know how I am about snow. I worry my fool head every time Geraldine has to drive in it. I'm glad I don't know what's going on where you live.

Mom never left home without makeup on and her hair done in the styles of the Hollywood stars she loved. She was always well groomed, a beautiful, colorful peacock. She took sewing classes at the local vocational school and became a skilled seamstress. She made stylish hats for herself and a sport coat for my father. She made many matching dresses with lots of smocking for Geraldine and me. She also made us Halloween outfits (one year we were Pilgrims—quite authentic looking), and she sewed an outfit for me when, at twelve years old, I appeared onstage at a youth club talent show.

As a young mother, Mom gave all her time to my sister and

me. She didn't get a job until we were teenagers. She cooked every meal and always baked cakes for our birthdays. She believed that everyone deserved a cake on his or her birthday. Later in my life, when my own kids and grandkids were small, she always asked, "Who made the cake?" I felt guilty if we had pie, which my mother considered inferior to cake. I wonder if her mother did the same. Maybe for Depression families, a cake was as good as it got.

As a treat and to get us out of the house (as youngsters, we seldom watched television), she often took us on outings to parks, zoos, and the beach, and we went to movies. I remember seeing *The Robe* in 1954. My nine-year-old self fell in love with Richard Burton, my first celebrity crush. I still love Rich, even though he is long gone from this earth. I've read three of his biographies.

Mom took us to see and meet John F. Kennedy. Kennedy campaigned in New Bedford during the 1952 US senatorial race. My mother, sister, and I walked to the municipal parking lot, where he was giving a speech. Standing on a dais so he could be seen, he drew a big crowd. Huddled in the cold, we were a ragtag-looking bunch bundled in our coats and hats with faces as pale as the moon, while he looked like a Greek god. In the middle of winter, he was golden tan, fit, hatless, and beaming the famous Kennedy grin. It was the beginning of a lifelong love affair between Massachusetts and the Kennedys. Mom proudly got his autograph, which eventually disappeared into the fabric of our house. Four years later, we sat around the kitchen table, listening to the Democratic National Convention on the radio. Kennedy had a surprisingly good showing, and we were rooting for him. In 1960, he was elected the first Catholic president of the United States. Then, as quickly as his star had risen, it was gone, and he was gone, faded into the mists of Camelot.

Mom often took my sister and me to Buttonwood Park, a wooded area with ponds, war memorials, baseball fields, and a small zoo. I have known this park all my life.

Ducks, geese, and other fowl lived near the duck pond, a water hole that ran under a small stone bridge. If a duck was clever, it could swim under the bridge and arrive at the other side, where there were no fences. Within the various fenced areas were grassy plains where deer, mountain goats, and two scraggly bison grazed. An old, grizzled grizzly bear lived by himself in a den built in the 1930s from large rocks. My sister and I thought he must be lonely. Finally, there was a monkey house, which also housed beautiful parrots.

In public, Mom preferred to be called Mother, but she settled for Mom. One name she disliked being called was Ma, and we rarely called her that. (Ironically, she called her own mother Ma.) But one day in the monkey house, my sister and I, without thinking, loudly called, "Hey, Ma!" to get her attention. "Hey, Ma!" repeated every parrot in the place over and over again in a riot of birdcalls. Mortified, Mom quickly slipped us out of the place before we could see if anyone was laughing. We knew Mom wasn't.

Mom was a nervous mother, and I was a nervous child. She had the trifecta of family neuroses: what are now known as obsessive-compulsive disorder, anxiety, and depression. The conditions were never officially diagnosed and likely were passed on to me. I sometimes wonder if our faith contributed to these problems. The threat of hell—a place of eternal damnation and endless flames, devils, and suffering—was scary. I was scared to death of mortal sins, which condemned one to hell. Missing Sunday Mass was a mortal sin. I was surprised the first time I missed Sunday Mass and lived to tell about it. I expected to go straight to hell. To make things more confusing, Catholics were taught that God was love and wanted you in heaven with him, yet you could be sent to hell for all eternity for once eating meat on Friday. That was a mixed message. As a young child, I was smart enough to sense the contradictions but young enough not to realize that the rules were made by men and could be faulty.

From an early age, I was anxious about my health and evolved into a bona fide hypochondriac. As a young adult, every headache was a brain tumor, shortness of breath was a heart attack, and a single drop of blood in my underwear was cancer. (Many girls thought they had cancer when they got their first period. I thought I had cancer every period.) I had everything checked immediately by an unsympathetic doctor. I could have used a little help for my anxiety, but at the time, mental problems were "all in your head." I was known as just a nervous child. Much later, Mom wrote,

> I'm not worried about your physical health, but you could end up with quite a case of nerves if you keep worrying.

Every Friday, as a much-needed break, my mother went to a movie with a girlfriend. My sister and I spent the night with our grandmother Nanny. When separated from my mother, I was a nervous wreck until she came home. I would wake from sleep, find her not there, and stand in the front window, looking for her. Even if I saw her outside talking with her friend, I would go back and forth from the bed to the window until she was back in the house. I discovered in a letter that she felt the same about me:

> I remember when Nanny took you to her church which was a rare occasion. I thought I would enjoy my time alone but I missed you. I couldn't wait until you got home.

Mom and I both had separation anxiety. I once wrote my mother a sad little letter when she had gone to Boston for a single day. I said how sad I was that she was gone, told her how much I missed her, and asked if she would please bring me home a toy.

Since Nanny didn't have a car, Mom occasionally took Nanny to visit the graves of her Norwegian relatives. Mom mentioned one visit:

Sunday I took Nanny to the cemetery in Fairhaven
& she saw all the graves she was interested in.
Your father would never think to take her around
like that & of course she wouldn't ask him.

Going to a Catholic school and taking religion seriously, I was
a spiritual little kid who believed in ghosts. I recall one terrifying
visit to a cemetery when I was three years old. It was a bright,
sunny day, but walking among the gravestones, I was scared and
didn't know why. I didn't know what was under the tombstones.
I didn't know what death was, only that it was frightening and
separated you from people you loved. I also didn't know what
ghosts were but thought that might be the day I would find out.
I was curious about a big stone mausoleum that had windows.
What could be seen inside? My mother picked me up so I could
find out. I expected to see dead people or ghosts inside, but I saw
only blackness. Mom and Nanny left the cemetery with memories,
and I left with questions about death, an exaggerated fear of
dying, and panic attacks. I got no help for my panic attacks. I was
thought of as a nervous child.

I first went to the dentist when I was three years old, and I
created such a scene that I was sent home. I had an uneasy feeling
all that day. After supper, my mother was reading me a book and
reassuring me that everything was fine, when I heard an ominous
knock on the door. It was the dentist. He laid me on the kitchen
table, knocked me out with ether, and fixed my teeth. My mother
had betrayed me. But I never held a grudge, and my teeth were fixed.

I didn't fare much better with dental care during grade
school. For years, my sister and I went to a dentist who didn't
use any numbing agents. The pain of a drill bit on a tooth nerve
is exquisite. My sister and I had high anxiety whenever we had
to see him. In addition to having no pain-relief medications, he
had no empathy for our discomfort, and he didn't have much of
a personality. We secretly called him the Butcher.

I went to kindergarten at the Cook School, which was across the street from our house. It was a square brick building with a brick wall around it. I used to walk around the building while balancing on the brick wall, never thinking I could fall. The entrance to kindergarten was at the top of a steep concrete stairway. We used to play dodgeball there with neighborhood kids. One of us would stand at the top of the stairs, and the others would stay at the bottom and try to pelt the one at the top with a small pink rubber ball.

In kindergarten, we were taught the basic ABCs and how to take a nap. I was a bright little kid and, as such, was asked to help produce graduation certificates. The certificates were simply folded pieces of paper. All I had to do was draw a *C* on the cover using a stencil and color it green. As it turned out, I drew every *C* upside down. I was humiliated. Furthermore, I failed napping. I was too energetic to nap, although I did manage to keep still.

My sister and I went to an Irish Catholic grade school taught by the Sisters of Mercy, an order of nuns founded in Ireland. The school was two short blocks from home. We walked in all kinds of weather. In our rain gear, we looked like the Gorton's Fisherman, with a bright yellow rain hat or helmet, a slicker (rain coat), and boots or rubbers. In the winter, we wore heavy snow pants under our dresses, and we were always bundled up in hat, scarf, coat, and mittens.

On my first day of elementary school, Father Murphy, always smiling, greeted me as I arrived. The three-story redbrick building was old, but the dark hardwood floors and stairways were newly varnished. My teacher was Sister Mary Protais. She was strict, and I didn't really warm up to her. But the school supplies were fascinating—papers and crayons and such. I loved them. I loved the smell of mimeographed paper. School was great! Before I left to go home, I slipped a crayon into my sweater—a thief on the first day of Catholic school. I thought I might be consigned to hell, but I brought the crayon home. I still love the smell of newly varnished floors; it reminds me of newness—a new school year, new things to learn, and new office supplies.

I made my First Communion on May 10, 1953. I know this because I still have my little white prayer book. Sister Mary Anne was my teacher, and I was in second grade. I was reading at a fourth-grade level, a minor prodigy. (Thank goodness I still had a love of learning in me after those upside-down *C*s in kindergarten.) In the fall, Sister asked us for news about the World Series. I liked her because she wanted to know what was going on in the world. I did too.

One day my third-grade teacher asked me to address some rumors she had heard about my behavior. I was eight years old and naive. I had no idea what she was talking about. It took Mom's intervention to straighten things out. The grandmother of one of my friends was spreading lies about my behavior. That was my first encounter with a bully, and it was somebody's grandmother. I had always loved grandmothers, so the whole thing was confusing to me. To this day, I don't know what motivated that mean-spirited grandmother to start rumors or even what the rumors were. They are sleeping dogs.

Throughout grade school, I had a good memory and a thirst for learning. I also had an artistic bent since we were taught art and music appreciation in addition to reading, writing, arithmetic, geography, and history. I became interested in acting when we put on plays. In fourth grade, I played the lead, Queen Isabella, in a play about the discovery of America.

We were also taught penmanship and letter writing: how to write different types of letters, how to address them, and so on. Letter writing is good for your brain. It teaches you to organize your thoughts and communicate them to others. I think of Mom's letters and wish these skills were still taught. But letter writing is a dying art.

Early on, although I was intelligent, I was the class clown. Making the other kids laugh was more important to me than getting As. My first few report cards displayed straight As, except for conduct, for which I earned a C. Mom was involved with my schoolwork. She was both encouraging and demanding. She expected, and accepted, nothing but straight As, including one for conduct. Mom encouraged competition with my peers. To this day, I remember the name of the girl who was my closest competitor in grade school. She was a pretty girl with finger curls and a bow in her hair. We both had averages in the nineties. The competition was usually over the decimal point. She and I knew we were competitors, but we never spoke of it. I wonder how her life turned out—if she went to college, married, or had children. In any case, I learned to control myself in class and was a straight-A student through ninth grade.

The nuns liked me. For one thing, I was a good student. But more importantly, whenever the nuns needed to go somewhere, usually to visit a convent in another city, I volunteered my mother to drive them. My mother, the nuns, my sister, and I drove all over the place. Mom chauffeured them cheerfully enough, although I suspected that at times, she wished I wasn't so free with my volunteering her services. But in my little-girl way of thinking, she had nothing better to do with her time than to shore up my favored-pupil status. We drove up and down the hills of Fall River and crossed the waters into Newport.

> I remember when you volunteered me to take the nuns to Providence & I got caught in a bad thunderstorm. I guess I was pretty hard on you for that but I had just gotten my license & was a nervous wreck.

I especially liked Sister Sheila, who taught seventh grade. She once gave me an A grade that I didn't deserve. I was conflicted about that. The grade saved me from a scolding from my mother, but I didn't earn it. Sister Sheila gave me the benefit of the doubt, and I was uncomfortable with it.

Since I went to a Catholic school, I studied religion from the Baltimore Catechism and went to Mass every day first thing in the morning. The teachings of the church were rich and deep and not open for discussion. My little soul was pure. When we students sat on our little wooden desk chairs, we left room for our guardian angels, who were there to protect and guide us.

I always liked the idea of a personal guardian angel, and I always believed I had a good, strong one who got me out of a lot of scrapes. Although Dad didn't believe in angels, he had a good one too, since he fell overboard a few times while fishing and was saved every time.

Once, when I was small, I heard a choir of angels singing. I was in the living room on a Sunday, and there was no one around. I distinctly heard singing. It sounded like it was coming from a church, but there were no churches near enough to explain it. I checked every room for radios and looked outside for passersby but found nothing. I came to the conclusion that it was a visit from the angels. It was the only time I ever heard them.

Later, I was puzzled by religion. I puzzled over why innocent babies couldn't go to heaven if they weren't baptized and why it was a mortal sin to miss Mass or eat meat on certain days. The God I believed in was warm and loving, not punitive. Later, I would further question my faith.

As a youngster, I took lessons in tap dancing, ballet, baton, piano, and drama and elocution. I especially enjoyed drama. Our group performed small skits at local venues, such as senior citizens' homes. I learned the elementals of stage presence—for example, to wear dark shoes when you appear onstage, because light shoes make your feet look big. Our teacher, Miss G., tried to take the New York accent out of my more proper New England one. I had to pronounce the word *cow* over and over to get out the twang. "Cow. Cow. Cow."

When I was ten years old, I got the mumps and was miserable and bedridden with the illness. Mom asked if I wanted her to get me anything. I asked for a potted fuchsia plant, a bleeding heart. I needed to feel close to the outside, where the world was busy while I lay sick in bed. Since I couldn't go outside, I brought the outdoors inside to me. The plant was my beacon of hope for a quick recovery. I hugged the pot in my sickbed and soon got better. Eventually, I got all the childhood diseases and gave them to my sister.

My sister and I witnessed Mom's temper. When we misbehaved, she threatened to send us to St. Mary's Home, a local orphanage, which we often saw when out walking. It looked like a big brick box and was ominous since we never saw children about the place. Were they locked inside? We took her threats seriously, not wanting to become orphans and live in a box. Although Mom never hit us, she often flicked a wet dishrag in our direction, and if it took purchase, so much the better. A mighty flick and a "Damn it to hell!" were her weapons of choice.

During my school years, in spite of my As, Mom often said I had little common sense, which was pretty much true. I was a dreamer. She often said to me, "Can't you do anything right?" Gosh, Mom, I was trying.

One day we were relaxing at home in the living room, and my sister and I asked Mom to tell us who she liked best. We asked that question a lot; sibling rivalry was high on our list of activities. Mom usually took some evasive action, but that day was different. She said casually, "I never wanted children." She added (not quite quick enough, in my opinion), "But once I had the two of you, I loved you." It was a stunning development. Mom never wanted children? In hindsight, my sister and I should have seen the signs. She never fussed over babies or gravitated toward little children. She ignored them. It wasn't out of the question that we were headed to St. Mary's Home!

As luck had it, my sister and I never got sent to the orphanage, and we continued to love Mom unconditionally, even if she hadn't wanted children. But I don't think we ever again asked her who her favorite was. We were thankful enough to be living with her.

Mom learned to drive when she was in her late twenties. My father taught her by driving with her. A so-called friend helpfully told Mom she had seen Dad driving with "another woman." Mom set the friend straight.

When Mom was a newly licensed driver, she was pulled over by a New York State trooper for driving too slow. The trooper asked her age, and when Mom told him she was twenty-nine, I started crying. "Mom, you told me you were sixteen!" I said, heartbroken that my mother was older than I'd thought. The trooper had a good laugh and let her off without a ticket. I was such a naive little kid—as was Mom, as she revealed in a letter:

> When I was 14, I still believed my mother was 16
> because she said so. What a dope I was.

You weren't a dope, Mom. You were a little girl.

Every Mother's Day, Mom said not to get her anything. Year after year, she said it. One year, Geraldine and I took her at her word. We thought we were doing the right thing. Big mistake. Mom was upset and angry. In the future, she said, "This time, I really mean it. Don't get me anything. I don't need anything." But we told her we weren't falling into that trap again. We got her gifts whether she wanted them or not.

Mom was from a generation who made good use of things. Everything was valuable; nothing was discarded. Her towels became so threadbare that light shone through them. Even at that stage, they weren't discarded. They were recommissioned as cleaning rags.

Usually, Mom didn't want to have house pets, but she loved the animals found in nature. She found a starving fox digging in her garden and bought it cans of cat food. She also fed leftovers to skunks, chipmunks, birds, and seagulls:

I finally threw out something the seagulls won't eat. I had some peanut butter kisses that no one was eating. I took the paper off & threw them out. The seagulls are out there now & acting very confused, they just sniff & fly away.

Your father and I saw a ferret convention on the news. One woman had 55 ferrets. They had them dressed in costumes and lots of them were trained to do tricks. They're cute but of course I wouldn't want one. I have my seagulls.

Another letter included this exchange about neighbors:

Our neighbor Mrs. H. asked Jeanette if she would stop feeding the birds. She said they were drawing mice & making a mess in her yard. It's probably the seagulls that I feed that are making the mess. I hope she doesn't ask me to stop.

In Kingston, there was always a cat around. Suzy was a scruffy old alley cat that lived outside. For a time, we had Fuzzy, a golden cocker spaniel. Fuzzy was a biter. He bit me and the mailman and earned himself a relocation. When we asked where he was, Mom said he went to live on a farm. We suspected Fuzzy went someplace more sinister, but we never knew for sure. Mom told us that when she was a child, our grandfather Pop drowned a litter of kittens in a sack in the Hudson River. Mom couldn't believe her father could do that, but it was a common method of pet disposal at the time. So whether Fuzzy went to the farm or the river, the result was the same: we never saw him again.

Mom was a cradle Catholic, born and raised in the faith. She went to Mass every Sunday and every day during Holy Week.

She prayed from a well-worn prayer book about an hour a day, for the living and the dead. She did good deeds, and she often went to confession.

During one of those confessions, she mentioned she had made a mistake by being matron of honor at a friend's Protestant wedding. Apparently, that was a sin. (I didn't know about sins adults could commit; I was focused on sins I could commit.) The priest told her she was excommunicated and said he would bring it up before the bishop. Two weeks passed before she heard from him—two weeks of agonizing fear for her. She was told the church would forgive the sin, but she must never, ever do it again without permission.

Mom felt relief. She never questioned the authority of the church or the many man-made rules added to the teachings of Christ. The pope was infallible in matters of faith. You could be sent to hell for eating meat on Friday or missing Sunday Mass. Even news about pedophiles didn't appear to shake her faith. She wrote,

> There was a picture of our priest in this morning's paper. He's accused of raping a boy in the 1960s. He had mass yesterday & he asked everyone to pray for him for a special intention. In a way I'm not too surprised because my neighbor told me years ago that he was transferred from one church to another because he liked little boys.

From the time I reached the age of reason at about seven years, I wondered what having faith felt like. The nuns told me that only Catholics went to heaven, and we were lucky to have been born into the faith. Did that mean my father wasn't going to heaven? Or my grandparents? That didn't seem fair.

Growing up, I went through all the proper motions of faith, attending Sunday Mass and Saturday confession, saying prayers, and observing the Holy Days. The nuns did such a good job of scaring their students that I believed in hell and knew with certainty that I didn't want to end up there. I believed that adherence to church teachings held sway over my afterlife, but I knew that God, if there was a God, had to be gentler and more forgiving than the church. I believe the church influenced my generalized anxiety. I was told I had faith when I couldn't feel it, and if I didn't have it, I couldn't go to heaven. Quite the conundrum.

Maybe I was an agnostic like Johnny Gunther, whose illness is the subject of the book *Death Be Not Proud*, written by his father, John Gunther Sr., which includes this quote from Johnny:

> Almighty God, Forgive me for my agnosticism; for I shall try to keep it gentle, not cynical, nor a bad influence. And O! If Thou art truly in the heavens, accept my gratitude for all Thy gifts and I shall try to fight the good fight.

From an early age, my sister had a strong Catholic faith. She never questioned it and went to Mass every week. She still does, and she sings in the choir. She told me she must have inherited the God gene. I eventually stopped going to church, although I still consider myself a spiritual person, and if asked to state my religion, I always say, "Catholic."

For a long time as a child, I felt as if I were an alien from out of this world. I sensed I was living with a foster family, and one day my real parents would come to claim me, shower me with love, and take me home This thinking calmed me during times when I was upset. The feeling didn't ever disappear, but it dissipated as I grew older and more in touch with who I was, or maybe I developed better ways to cope with feelings of detachment.

I had emotional issues from a young age. Dad wasn't really present in my life, and Mom was highly demanding. She scolded me and often said, "You can't do anything right." It hurt me a lot when she said that, and I hated myself for disappointing her. I knew my parents loved me; I just didn't feel it—sort of like the faith I was born into.

In one of her letters, Mom wrote,

> I got to thinking I never tell you I love you & I do.

When I read that Mom loved me, I was shocked—not that she did but that she said she did. We were a family who never talked about feelings or emotions. We never hugged or kissed the way some families do. However, as long as we avoided any uncomfortable topics, Mom was easy to talk to, and we talked on the phone at least weekly. In fact, she was on the phone a lot, talking to her family, her friends, and neighbors. Mom was friendly and outgoing; she liked people and enjoyed listening to their stories. She sent dozens of greeting cards and letters and received dozens in return.

Mom tried hard to be a good mother, and for the most part, I had a happy childhood. I always felt safe. But Mom worried about me too much to enjoy my early years. She shielded me from as many dangers as she could. Consequently, I was book smart but ignorant about life, a protected innocent—and the world was creeping in. I was starting to tire of competing for grades in school, I resented having to go to Mass each week, my ego was starting to take a beating, and I thought I came from outer space. As I grew from child to teenager, the signs were all there: I would face problems in the years ahead of me.

CHAPTER 3

My Old Man and the Sea

My first word was *Dada*, and in my first photograph, my father holds me in his arms. He is handsome and smiling widely, as if I am the light of his life. We are in the backyard of the house on Hanratty Street, and although the photo is in black and white, I can tell the sun is shining.

The sea was in my father's blood. He was born on the rocky island of Karmøy, Norway. The sea around Karmøy is dangerous, filled with underwater currents, and its seabed is filled with rocks. People have lived on Karmøy since the Stone Age. Burial mounds and stone monuments dot the island. The first king of a unified Norway, the Viking Harald Fairhair, lived there.

In 1919, my father was born on the Vikre family farm and named Knut Knutsen. The name Knut is from the Old Norse meaning "bold one." For at least five generations, his great-grandfathers—all named Knut Knutsen—grew small amounts of crops on the farm and fished for herring in the surrounding seas. It was dangerous work, and one great-grandfather drowned, along with his oldest son. The Vikre men descended from the early kings of Norway, their descent long forgotten.

Dad and his father were fishermen like their ancestors. They immigrated to America and fished the deep seas off the coast of Massachusetts. Ironically, although Dad was a fisherman all his life and it was the only job he knew, he hated it. I once told him how much I liked my job, and he said I was lucky because most people hated their jobs. Mom wrote of him,

> He hated fishing. It must have been hard to spend your life doing something you hated, but he did retire young so he had that. He was only 57 when he retired.

Norwegians are a proud people. They are strong, stoic, and unmoving like the rocks they live on. My father was destined to be a fisherman. It was his heritage. In a modern world removed from the time and place in which he was born, he might have had a different life. He loved reading and learning new things. I can see him as a college professor, much liked by his students, wearing a camel-colored sport coat with suede patches on the elbows and carrying books and lesson plans. He might have taught philosophy.

Since it was hard to make a living on the rocky island of Karmøy, my grandfather left Norway and immigrated to New York. He got a job rum-running for an organization owned by Al Capone. My grandmother kept home in Norway while my grandfather worked and saved money to bring his family to America. It took seven years.

While in Norway, Dad managed on his own from an early age, running errands for his mother from the tender age of two. His mother, busy with Dad's infant brother, followed his little red cap from the window as he did his chores. It was the only part of him that could be seen. Dad had a dog named Flinke, which means "clever." When Dad was two years old, he waded into the sea and kept going deeper. Clever Flinke pulled him back, possibly saving his life and making mine possible. Good boy, Flinke.

Dad had one brother, Jakob, who was younger but close in age. Shortly after Christmas in 1923, Jakob became ill with meningitis. Getting a doctor was out of the question. There were no phones and no means of transportation in the heavy snows. My grandmother did the only thing she could do: she held him. He looked up at her and said, "Mama, I'm so tired," and he died.

In America, my grandfather received a cable informing him of the death of his oldest son, Knut. He knew that wasn't true because he had dreamed about the death of his youngest son, Jakob.

After Jakob died, my grandmother put Dad on a pedestal. He could do no wrong. Consequently, he expected service like a king for much of his life.

My father and his mother immigrated to America when he was ten years old. He claimed he had the best food of his life on the steamship. He must have been hungry, because his mother was an excellent cook. He caught measles onboard, didn't miss a meal, and was well enough to pass the health exam at Ellis Island.

My father went to school in Brooklyn and completed the eighth grade. In his teens, he joined the merchant marines. Later, he moved to New Bedford, where his parents had settled. He took work on commercial fishing vessels. His father, who was also a fisherman, helped him find boats that needed crew members. When World War II broke out, he joined the Army Air Force. He was stationed at Stewart Air Force Base in upstate New York, where he met and married my mother. During the war, he served as a mechanic. Years later, Mom wrote,

> After work tonight, your father wants me to go shopping with him. He has a list of things he wants to get. One of them is a device to lift the car so you can work under it. What he wants that for, I'll never know. When the car needs work, He brings it to a garage.

This letter amuses me. Dad fixed airplanes during the war but didn't fix his own cars.

Dad's father loved babies and little children. He gave them horsey rides on his back and bounced them on his knee. He played the fiddle. Like my father, my grandfather smoked for much of his life and drank when he was younger. His death, though not unexpected, was sudden. He died from lung cancer not long after being diagnosed. I flew to his funeral with my first daughter and an unborn child whose birth my grandfather had been looking forward to. When the child arrived a few months later with platinum-blonde hair and blue eyes, Dad's mother called her Norwegian Tracey. At the funeral, I met neighbors, and we started to talk and laugh. My dad approached me. In a soft voice, he asked me to please be quieter. His father was being laid to rest, and reverence was called for. I remember the sad look on my father's face. He was quietly grieving, and I was laughing with the neighbors. I was embarrassed and obeyed my dad. I was learning compassion.

My mother and her mother-in-law were close but not affectionate. They got along for Dad's sake.

> Nanny went to the doctor for a check-up. She has had a lump in her breast for some time. She has to have the whole breast removed. Poor thing has had her share of operations, but like she said, "I can't lay down & die." She didn't seem upset about it. Your father thinks she's proud of it because it's a challenge, but I said, "Are you kidding? Nobody wants to have an operation to prove that they are up to a challenge." I think she puts on a big front so he won't get upset.

Although Nanny had many health problems, including tuberculosis, a bad bout of shingles, impaired hearing, cancer, and several surgeries, she died suddenly at home with no evidence of fear or pain on her face. Dad found her. She had been reading the newspaper. We never knew what killed her, but what did it matter? She was gone from our lives. I called Dad in tears to tell him I wouldn't be able to come to the funeral. He quickly handed the phone to Mom. Dad didn't like dealing with emotions.

Fishing was Dad's only job and his livelihood. He hated it, but he was good at it. He advanced from crew member to captain to boat owner–captain and finally to boat owner. Dad was well liked by his fellow fishermen in the New Bedford fishing fleet. It seemed most of them knew him. Years after he retired, he would occasionally run into an old-timer from the docks, and they would catch up on the fishing news. He was elected president of the Seafood Producers Union for several years in the 1970s. One time, I flew home to see him sworn in. It was a proud moment for me to see my father recognized by his industry.

As kids, my sister and I would go to Fisherman's Pier with my mother to watch my father's boat chug out of the harbor on a fishing trip or to await its return. I knew I was on the pier when the air smelled like fish and seaweed and the seagulls glided and cawed overhead. You could drive on the paved pier and park near the moored boats. We played on the pier, skipping about the big wooden pilings, careful not to skip into the water, which was deep enough to float a fishing boat and dirty with diesel slicks. My father let us come aboard his boat. To come aboard, you jumped from the pier to the boat. Since the boat was tethered to a piling by a thick rope, it had room to drift farther from the pier, and sometimes it was a dauntingly long jump. We explored the boat, noting the small bunks and kitchen and the cabin my father steered the boat from.

Dad fished the Georges Bank area of the Atlantic Ocean, about seventy miles offshore. The boat left its pier in New Bedford and motored to the fishing area. They fished for halibut, haddock, yellowtail, and cod on a boat that was called a dragger because the fishing nets were dragged through the water. For a while, when he owned his boat, he tried lobstering, which required changes to the configuration of the boat. Lobstering was expensive because of the cooling requirements to keep the lobsters alive. After a short time, he returned to dragging, which afforded a better chance to make money.

My father fished year-round in two-week cycles. Each trip took two weeks, followed by a few days at port, during which time the boat was restocked and repaired if needed. My father was home only infrequently. In effect, Mom raised my sister and me as if she were a single mother.

Dad's sense of time was out of sync with ours. Ours was the typical five-day school week followed by the weekend, with church on Sunday. His was a two-week fishing trip followed by a few days at home. He didn't attend church, although he was nominally a German Lutheran.

Sometimes in the winter, Dad's boat would arrive at port completely encased in foot-thick ice. Fishing was hard work; you were at the mercy of the elements, and occasionally, a boat didn't return home. It was crushed or sunk by a savage storm. Fishermen fell overboard, got tangled in netting, or drowned for some other reason. Dad fell overboard a few times. He was thrown a ring and quickly saved. My father was a fisherman who couldn't swim, but he said that swimming wouldn't save you in the deep sea waters miles from land. Since the 1920s, more than three hundred men have died while fishing from New Bedford boats, and their bodies were rarely found.[1] In the time when my father was fishing, he personally knew all the captains who were lost. They were men in the prime of their lives, and their deaths left many widows and fatherless children.

---

[1] "Lost Fishermen From the Port of New Bedford," accessed May 15, 2020, http://www.lostfishermen.com

When the haul, or catch, of fish arrived back at shore, men called lumpers unloaded the boat and took the fish to the auction house, which was right on the pier. How much money a fishing trip made depended on how many pounds of each type of fish had been caught and the daily price for a pound of that fish, as determined by consumer need. Representatives from the city's fish-processing plants bid on the fish. If you had a good catch of cod and the price of cod was high, you had a good trip. If you had a good catch but the price was low, you didn't. It was a fickle industry.

Mom listened to the fishing news on the local radio station every morning at 8:50 a.m., especially when my father's boat came in. The news gave each boat's haul—how much fish by type of fish—and the prices they sold for at auction, so she could estimate how much money Dad would bring home. He was a good provider. Mom got every check, except one or two when he got mugged before coming home from a fishing trip. Life was dangerous on the piers as well as at sea.

I found out long after my father died that he had a reputation for being the last one to come into port during a storm—after all, he was the bold one. Apparently, he was like Billy Tyne, the captain of the doomed ship in *The Perfect Storm*. I worried about him constantly, and many of my dreams were nightmares that his ship had gone down. My mother worried too. She often wrote about the dangers of fishing in her letters:

> A fishing boat, the *Navigator*, was lost at sea with 13 men. It made contact with another boat on Nov. 30 and was never heard from again. The skipper was a friend of your father. It's a terrible Xmas for the families.
>
> There's a fishing boat missing, the *Irene and Hilda*, they think it went down in the storm. They're still

looking for it. Your father knows the skipper, he
said he was about his age.

I think those fishermen from the *Lady of Grace* are
gone. They found the boat in Nantucket Sound,
it had sunk in severe winter weather. No bodies
were found.

I'm reading *The Perfect Storm* & thinking so much
of your father.

Yes, Dad was another Billy Tyne.

After coming home from a fishing trip, the crews cashed their
paychecks and headed to the bars. My father was no exception.
He almost always came home drunk after a trip. While we were
glad he survived the trip, we were also nervous about his return.
He was a mean drunk, so my sister and I hid from him until he
sobered up. Once, in a state of inebriation, Dad told my sister and
me that we were "the fruit of his loins," and he tried to hug us,
which was very much out of character for him. The behavior was
so strange that it scared us, and we ran out of the house. We didn't
come back until he was sober, and there was no more talk of loins.

Dad's drinking went on for years, but he only drank when the
boat came in, and he was not without ambition. For a fisherman,
the greatest achievement was owning your own boat. In 1964, my
father and a partner built the *Falcon*, one of the first steel-hulled
boats in the New Bedford fishing fleet. Previously, boats had
wooden hulls. In fact, there was a wooden-hulled *Falcon* that had
been sold for oceanographic research. A diner in Rhode Island
displays a lifeboat from the old *Falcon*.

At the new *Falcon*'s launch in Bristol, Massachusetts, Mom
and the partner's wife each christened the boat with a bottle
of champagne. I stood nearby, smiling proudly at my parents.
The seventy-five-foot boat slowly slid into the water. I had goose

bumps as it became waterborne. Then it belonged to the sea. For my parents, the boat was both their means of livelihood and, later, an albatross around their necks. The boat was part of the family; its successes were ours, as were its failures. A broken-down ship made no money.

For years, the boat enabled my father to make a good living. At first, my father was captain-owner. After he retired from active fishing at the age of fifty-seven, he hired the captains to take the boat on its fishing trips. Unfortunately, my father's skill in landing good catches of fish didn't transfer to the captains he hired. The boat started to lose money, mainly due to mechanical problems but sometimes due to poor decisions made by the captains, such as deciding to return to port for a storm that didn't materialize.

> The *Falcon* was in over the weekend. For the past couple of trips, it's been doing well, thank goodness. For the first 6 months of this year, it did so poorly your father was thinking of selling his half.

At that time, although my father had retired from fishing, he was still responsible for the boat and its finances. Due to an accounting error, Mom and Dad inadvertently got in trouble with the IRS. The IRS claimed the boat hadn't paid $80,000 in taxes. The tax liability was handled by the ship's accountant, who committed suicide when the tax issue surfaced. I didn't know how serious the problem was until I heard that someone had taken his life over it. My father often paced the floors in the early morning hours until the issue was settled. It was a troubled time for my family; we all wondered if we would lose our house because of the boat. The *Falcon* had become an albatross. My parents worried about the IRS problem for years until there was a settlement. Afterward, the boat continued to have problems. Mom wrote,

Every time they get ready to go out something else breaks down. Your father is really disgusted. Those fellows that work on it are like the guys that work on cars. Sometimes they make it worse. They fix one thing & break another.

The boat was finally put on the market. Mom wrote,

The boat has been for sale for over a year now & they haven't had a nibble. Just last week I decided to start a novena to St. Jude. Well! This morning the agent called and he might have a buyer. It seems too good to be true but it's the first nibble we've had.

The boat sold later that year for one-fifth of the original asking price. Although the *Falcon* didn't sell for much, it had served my parents well. It had paid its debts and owed us nothing. Thanks to Dad's business sense, his skills as ship captain, and Mom's skills at saving money, the *Falcon* put the family in a good place financially. We weren't rich, but we always could afford what we needed. With the sale of the boat, my father retired from fishing for good.

At home, my father lived a solitary and sedentary life. His greatest happiness came when he was alone, reading his books or drawing in his doodle book. His doodle book is an amazing creation—about four hundred pages of drawings he created in detail on scrap paper. I can't look at his doodles without wondering what he had in mind.

He created what I believe are other worlds.

He drew in this book in any spare time he had, when he wasn't reading. I consider his book a work of art. In some things, Dad was frugal, and he didn't believe in buying drawing paper. His beautiful doodles are drawn on used newsletters. His artistry and imagination shine through on printouts from business meetings.

In 1950s America, it was a mother's job to stay home and raise the kids. Fathers earned the income. The boundaries were clear. Consequently, Dad wasn't closely involved in my upbringing. Although he was highly intelligent, he never knew the date of my sister's or my birthday. One time, when I was talking to him on the phone, I mentioned that I had just had a birthday. It embarrassed him that he didn't know. He blamed my mother for not telling him before he talked to me.

> Yesterday I was having raspberries for dessert & I put some in a dish for your father. When I picked it up, I dropped it & had berries all over my clothes, the refrigerator (that I had just cleaned), & all over the kitchen floor. What a mess. Your father said I was being punished for not telling him it was your birthday. He said that was my job.

I have a memory of being at a school football game and looking into the sky, wondering what would happen if my father were to die. When I was sixteen, I faced the possibility of my father not living through an operation he had to have on the veins in his leg. The doctors gave him fifty-fifty odds to survive. A friend of his needed the same operation, and my father talked him out of it. The fellow died. But the time wasn't right for Dad to die. He survived the operation and somehow managed not to miss a single meal in the hospital. He worked for another fifteen years after his surgery. By that time, I was married and raising children of my own.

Dad had been a heavy smoker of unfiltered cigarettes since he joined the merchant marines as a teenager. His fate was sealed early. He quit smoking only when, later in life, he developed emphysema, which caused him to have breathing problems.

After he quit smoking, he tended to his health. He was a different man. Dad took all kinds of multivitamins, supplements, and specialty products, such as saw palmetto for prostate health. He had entire bookshelves filled with pill bottles. He never drank alcohol. He also loved gadgets; he had a VitaMix juicer, a blood-pressure tester, and even an infrared wand for putting heat on sore muscles.

> Your father is waiting for me, he wants to go shopping. It's only 8:30 AM & he has all day, but he's ready. He's getting like an old lady now. He watches the paper for sales, etc. He came home with $75 worth of vitamins & a few other things. He's busy reading *Life Extension* by Durk Pearson who claims he's going to live to be 140.

He faithfully read *Prevention Magazine* and self-help books. Dad was convinced he would live to be one hundred years old. Mom reported,

> Your father is now drinking vinegar & water every day. He thinks he's going to live to reach 100. More power to him!

Dad was six feet tall and weighed well over two hundred pounds. He spoke like an American, with not a trace of a Norwegian accent, and he used perfect grammar. He spoke Norwegian with his parents and did all his mental math in Norwegian. His handwriting was beautiful—small and fine, with an italic slant and a few flourishes. For a time, he started using the patois of the docks, peppering his speech with *dis* and *dat* (*dis* person or *dat* guy). Mom asked why he was speaking like that, and he said he wanted to be understood. That didn't last long. He was a perfectionist by nature.

He would have won no Husband of the Year awards, but he was much loved by his children. If he was angry or frustrated, he said, "Good night!" It became his signature phrase and one he is remembered for. He never swore, not once that I remember. Mom once referred to him as "a brute of a man," but I believe he was a gentleman at heart. He might not have known my birthday, but he never threatened to send me to an orphanage. In fact, he never criticized me. The only harsh words he ever said to my sister and me were "Keep quiet!" when we sang in the car or got into a fit of giggles when he was driving.

At home, Dad could be hard on my mother. He was stubborn and demanding. One evening at dinner, my mother noticed he wasn't eating and asked him what was wrong. He replied that he didn't have a fork. Shaking her head, my mother got up from the table and got him a fork.

My sister also found him stubborn, and they often argued. He never budged from a point of view, even if my sister had the better one. I had moved out of state and had few opportunities to argue with him.

He had little talent for tinkering with things and got frustrated easily. Once, during a visit when I was in my thirties, I asked him to put some kites together for my kids. He tried and tried but couldn't do it. Instead of letting it go, he went into a rage. We all left the room. I was so sorry I had asked him to do it. When he became frustrated like that with something Mom had asked him to do, she gave him a wide berth. Occasionally, his projects were successful. He made a stick to pick up litter, like the ones prisoners use, and he was proud as punch.

He liked to play *Jeopardy* along with the contestants when it came on TV. As intelligent as he was, he didn't have quick recall, and when my sister and I blurted out the answers before him, he left the room in frustration. We never bit our tongues to give him time to come up with an answer. Shame on us.

Mom did most of the cooking, and she was a fine cook. After

my sister and I left home, she invited my sister and her family to dinner every Sunday for years. Dad liked to cook, but generally, nobody ate his food. For example, he made healthy scones that were loaded with fruit, nuts, and bran and were as heavy as hockey pucks. But he made the best mashed potatoes. They were better than Mom's. He added only salt, pepper, and evaporated milk. Then he whipped them until they were soft and creamy. He boasted about how good his potatoes were every time he made them. Mom had no comeback. She agreed with him. These little things kept them friendly.

> Your father is making the mashed potatoes for Thanksgiving. The only thing I don't like about that is I'll have to clean the walls, the counter, etc. But it will be worth it. His mashed potatoes are much better than mine.

At dinner, Mom waited on him, and he expected good service. When dining out, he was demanding of the waitstaff. Mom was embarrassed if he treated them like servants. As good a cook as Mom was, Dad usually found fault with everything she made. One day he reached into the kitchen pantry to find something for breakfast. He found a plastic container filled with what he thought was granola. He put some granola in a bowl, added milk, and ate it. When Mom saw what he had just eaten, she told him that it was dry food for Geraldine's dog. My father ate a bowl of dog food. When Mom asked him how it was, he said, "Not bad." The dog food got no complaints, whereas Mom's exemplary cooking always did.

Although he lived in America, where everyone bought American cars, my Norwegian dad bought European cars for much of his life. He believed they were built better than American cars. After my sister wrecked his dark blue Humber imported from England, he bought a series of Hillmans, small cars also from England. He was about to buy a new Hillman, when my sister and I talked him into buying a 350Z Chevrolet Camaro, a car with lots of horsepower. We were in our college years and wanted a hot car to impress the boys. We couldn't believe Dad got it, and he soon wished he hadn't. It didn't have the features he liked: compact size and good gas mileage. Plus, my mother couldn't drive it. It was too big and powerful for her. After a short period of unhappy ownership of this sole American car, Dad switched to German cars. He bought Golfs or Jettas for the rest of his life. They were reliable, plain, and European.

On the road, my father was a notoriously bad driver. He drove fast on city streets and slow on freeways. He ignored traffic signs and lights of all colors. During a trip to Boston when I was a child, I thought we would all die in a car wreck. He drove through red lights and stop signs. "They shouldn't be there!" he said. He passed cars as if he were driving a Formula One car: fast and with quick lane changes. There was no reasoning with him. He said that while driving among aggressive drivers, you had to become one. During the Boston trip, I nervously shredded a facial tissue into dust, but we made it home without a scratch. I don't remember Dad ever getting a ticket in a lifetime of aggressive driving. But I never outgrew my fear of driving with him, even when I was an adult.

Although their garden was very small, Mom and Dad loved to garden. Usually, Mom planted flowers, and Dad planted the vegetables. Occasionally, they planted weeds. Mom described their plantings as follows:

> Geraldine has some pretty flowers in her yard. I dug around & took a small stalk of what I thought was one of them. I've been nurturing & watering it & even staked it because it drooped. This weekend I found out I've been nurturing a weed.

When I got back from visiting you, your father
had a big weed planted in a flowerpot outside.
He didn't know what it was, but he thought it
looked good.

They contended with critters:

Something has been digging up all my flowers.
It's happened about 4 times now. I'm not going to
bother any more, the animal is smarter than I am.
I surrounded the plants with rocks & the animal,
or whatever, was able to move the rocks.

The rabbits have done a good job on the veggies
& now there's a new crop of rabbits.

Dad would buy all his vegetables when they went on sale and
immediately plant them. His garden was in the ground in April in
Massachusetts, which can have frost or even snow well into May.
My mother always told him it was too early to plant, but he said
the stores wouldn't have sold the plants if it wasn't the right time
for planting. Every year, he lost some plants to frost, and every
year, he planted them in April. He was as stubborn as an ox.

After I moved to Ohio, whenever I talked to Dad on the phone,
he was always happy to talk about his garden, even if he didn't
have one planted when I called. He was close to nature and loved
growing things. I can see him as a gentleman farmer after retiring
from his imaginary teaching career.

Conversations with Dad were awkward, but I talked to him
every week. When I called Mom, Dad always answered the phone
for a brief chat. The topics I could readily discuss with him were
the weather and his garden. He never initiated a topic, only
commented; he wasn't a conversationalist. However, he was the
smartest man I knew.

He read voraciously; his favorite genre was science fiction, and he bought so many paperbacks he had duplicates and triplicates of many. When he went book shopping, he came back with bags full; he read so many he didn't know what he had read and what he hadn't, so he bought all of them that were on display. He read the *Encyclopedia Britannica* cover to cover four times and held a wealth of knowledge in his head. Mom always said Dad had lots of book smarts but little common sense. For example, on his seeing his granddaughter Leanne perform in a play, Mom wrote,

> Your father and I went to see Leanne in her play last Fri. One little girl was very good, she was a regular little actress. But considering how shy Leanne is, she did very well. After the play was over, your father said, "How come you couldn't do as well as Melanie?" Geraldine and I jumped on him. Honestly! He thinks he's so smart, but that was a dumb thing to say.

Mom sent what I considered an interesting letter about Dad's barbershop:

> Your father just walked to get his hair cut. He has this barber who is a real character. He's into music & he has all kinds of records that he plays & he also sings. He has a Jewish customer who's a survivor of the Holocaust & he comes & chats. Where your father fits in is anybody's guess.

Dad never did quite fit in anywhere. He was a fisherman and a scholar. After Dad retired, he was always reading or drawing doodles. He wasn't an overtly loving person, but he was much loved. He didn't know my birthday or my sister's, but we knew his and celebrated it every September. To this day, we never fail to note the date. Mom always made him a strawberry cream cake, her specialty, for his birthday: homemade pound cake with fresh strawberry topping and hand-whipped cream. We always tried to find presents he would like. I often gave him vitamins and trail mix. Geraldine tried to find him useful and interesting gifts, which he sometimes didn't appreciate. He was hard to please.

As children, Geraldine and I never competed for his attention, because he gave his attention equally—a small amount to only a few people. Any time he paid attention to either of us was a joy.

If my father had wanted a boy, he did just as well with me. As a child, I played with toy soldiers and tanks, cowboys and forts, and trucks. I loved trucks. He built me a wooden garage with car lifts that went up and down. I was thrilled that he made it for me. I was impressed with the garage and proud of Dad's craftsmanship.

As a young adult, I had a small leather-covered chest purchased at Waterbeds 'n' Stuff. He didn't think the leather was in great condition, so he polished it and then buffed it. Afterward, I was so proud of that chest. It had caught Dad's eye, and he made it beautiful for me. Today my grandson has the chest.

I loved my father, but I never told him. Of course, he never told me he loved me either.

Dad never played with us, but he showed us how much pleasure reading and drawing could be. He wasn't formally educated, but he was highly intelligent, and his intellect challenged ours. He wasn't a religious man. I asked him, "What happens after we die?" and he said, "Nothing happens. We stop living, and that's it." Because I thought of my father as the smartest man I knew, when he said there was no afterlife, I listened. Looking back, I believe his words had an impact on me, and he bolstered the seed of doubt I had about my faith. I hope Dad found out he was wrong.

Dad and I were dreamers. When I was small, I loved to draw, and I created entire towns with my drawings. I would draw people in families; give them names and ages; and then draw their houses, others in the town, streets, and buildings. I would make up stories about the families. Maybe he did the same as he worked in his doodle book.

Dad was a man of few words but deep thoughts. I wish I had pried those thoughts from him. Dad might have had faults, but he was never a silly person or unreasonable. I could have learned more from him than I did.

If I could live my life over, I would have talked to both Dad and Mom more often. I would have chewed their ears off asking for information about their childhoods, how they felt about things, and what they were interested in. I would have been a chatterbox, constantly probing, discovering, and getting to know them. These opportunities are lost. I wish I had been a better daughter.

Dad lived a hard life on the sea. He spent most of his retirement sitting in his recliner and reading. He was an intelligent man with few emotions, but he was a kind and gentle father, and his children loved him.

CHAPTER 4

Hey, Little Sister

I was an only child for only two years. I was still getting to know my mother when my sister was born and I lost my only-child status. Mom thought I needed company. Now I had a competitor. My mother named her Geraldine, which I pronounced as Jelly Bean, so in her early years, she was called Beanie, a name she now dislikes. When she was born, I didn't see her as a gift from my parents. I saw her as an interloper, and I bit her big toe. I thought she would take my mother away from me. In reality, she taught me how to share my mother. When my sister arrived, Mom and Dad argued over her name. He wanted to give her a Norwegian name, Ardis. Rather than continue the fight, Dad left home for a few days. To punish him for leaving, Mom named her Geraldine after her brother Gerard and the saint.

She was the cutest baby I ever saw, with a perfectly round face, brown eyes, wavy hair, and a big smile. Over the years, I grew to love her as Mom did; she is mentioned in almost every one of Mom's twelve hundred letters.

My first fully formed memory in my life is of my little sister. She is standing on the sidewalk in front of our house on Chestnut Street, holding a balloon. She is a toddler, wearing a shell-pink corduroy jacket-and-pants set with a matching bonnet. The balloon comes in contact with the thorns on the Japanese barberry bushes and bursts, and she starts to cry. I feel sorry for her because her balloon has burst. I am three years old.

From that tender start, we went on to have a typical sibling relationship, full of sharing and scrapping, ups and downs.

At a young age, my sister had a few crazy adventures. Once, Mom and Dad were getting ready to have a rare evening out. Looking for a little help, Mom asked Dad to give my sister some water. Geraldine was about six months old and barely able to sit. He handed her a glass of water, which she immediately spilled all over herself and the crib, making a mess for Mom to clean.

Another time, Dad was driving too fast around a corner, and my sister fell out of the car. Seat belts were unheard of then. Apparently, so were locked doors.

When Geraldine was two, she was bitten by a dog while out for a walk with Nanny, our grandmother. Nanny stopped to talk to a neighbor, and Geraldine, who sat in a stroller, dangled her hand by a white picket fence behind which a black Scottish terrier stood. The dog bit her fingers, and she was taken to the emergency room, where she got stitches. Later in life, Mom told her that her little finger was almost severed. Who couldn't love a toddler who had so many mishaps before she was even three years old?

I had my own share of adventures. One Sunday, Nanny was looking after baby Geraldine and three-year-old me while Mom went to eleven o'clock Mass. The baby was getting all the attention. I didn't mind; I made plans. I decided to walk about two miles to Buttonwood Park. All I had to do was open the door, and I was out. Accompanied by Steven, a neighbor my age, I left on my journey through the neighborhoods. When Mom got back from church, she realized I was missing and called the police. I was found six hours later, hungry and disheveled. Steven and I had come upon a small group of ruffians who stole my coat and a pretty brooch I was wearing. My hair was a mess. A kind lady who lived in the neighborhood saw the two of us walking alone and being hassled by the ruffians and called the police. The police drove us home. Later, Steven wasn't allowed to play with me, since the adventure had been my idea. Mom was too relieved to be angry and said Steven would follow anyone anywhere.

Until we started school and found our own friends, my sister and I were best friends. She began where I left off; we were like peas in a pod. I was the stereotypical oldest child in an American family: the adventurer and risk-taker. I made mistakes. As the youngest child, Geraldine learned from my mistakes and was calmer and better behaved than I was.

I was a whiny, demanding child, complaining about everything both at home and out on the town. Around the time I started school, Mom and I stopped at a drugstore. A neighbor noted my behavior, which had improved, and said, "She's not as whiny now, is she?" Mom was incensed and didn't appreciate the comment. In her eyes, I was perfection, even if I was whiny.

As youngsters, my sister and I were highly competitive for Mom's attention, although we called it different names—for example, "Mom, Geraldine won't give me my pencil!" or "Mom, Kathy took my paper doll!" We were like cats growling before the fight, circling each other for the advantage—and we did fight. We fought like cats and dogs. We got all twisted up in knots, a combination of fighting and wrestling. Sometimes it felt as if we were fighting to the death, but since we both lived, I have to assume we didn't go all out. I never once remember being injured from the fights. Eventually, we put aside the sibling rivalry and formed tight bonds. We survived.

As small children, we dressed alike in clothes Mom had made. All our early photos show us wearing matching dresses. We started dressing differently when we started school.

My sister and I went to the same grade school, played together, and took trips together. We sat together in the backseat during the family car rides to and from Kingston. Although our singing and giggling annoyed my father, we loved to sing while on the road, and we both loved spending the summer in Kingston. We read horror comic books, among others. They were gruesome even by today's standards, yet we read them cover to cover.

Geraldine had beautiful, thick, curly hair, while mine was straight and baby-fine. I always liked her hair better than mine. As I mentioned, we saw *The Robe* when we were children. Afterward, my mother braided Geraldine's hair around a sprig of white flowers in the style worn by Jean Simmons in the movie. I was highly envious because I didn't have hair that could be styled in any fashion. My sister was so pretty.

When I was ten, Dad got us brand-new Schwinn Tiger bicycles. Mine was red, and my sister's was green. They were state-of-the-art three-speeds. We learned to ride them on the Cook School playground, which was paved, and we rode them all around the neighborhood. Bike riding gave us our first sense of freedom. When I pedaled so fast that the breeze blew my hair back, I felt like nothing could stop me. I became an excellent rider. Thanks to a good sense of balance, I could stand on the seat while the bike was coasting. I was always proud of my athletic maneuvers on a bike.

When we got older and didn't want to dress alike, we went to the Star Store to shop for clothes. The store had magical vacuum tubes for transferring money. They whooshed all over the place. When we tried on new shoes, our feet were viewed with a fluoroscope, an x-ray device. You could see your skeletal toes within the shoe and judge if you had a good fit. Was getting irradiated by x-rays a reasonable price to pay for a good-fitting shoe? By the 1970s, the machines were banned because of health concerns.

We both wore brown-and-white saddle shoes. My sister remembers wearing flouncy skirts with fuzzy appliquéd poodles. I had a penchant for handbags and got a new one with every change of season. Shopping at the Star Store was a fun experience, and our memories of it are good.

Geraldine and I attended Holy Family Elementary School, which was a short two-block walk from our home. She also attended Holy Family High School, but I transferred to a public school in tenth grade. Her grades, including conduct, were always good. Mom didn't have to push her because Mom knew she always did her best.

My sister and I wanted pets of any and all kinds, but caring for them wasn't our forte. That duty fell to my mother. Mom loved animals, and she passed that love along to Geraldine and me. But she didn't necessarily want to live with animals. Once, we had baby turtles with painted shells. My mother, while housecleaning, set their bowl on the radiator while she dusted, and she forgot about them. They cooked to death when the heat came on. It was a sad lesson in pet responsibility. Mom was busy cleaning. I should have taken care of the poor turtles.

Tiger was a beautiful orange-striped cat. Mom, Geraldine, and I loved him. He was a fine fellow, and there was something special about him. He was allowed to live in the house. He traveled to Kingston with us one summer and got distemper, and we had to leave him there. Our grandfather Pop took him to the vet, but he couldn't be saved. We were heartbroken and grieved for Tiger, our sweet boy.

Once, for a short time, a tiny black puppy named Inky came into our lives. Mom had relented and allowed us to get a dog. But as a puppy, he was destructive, not housebroken, and quite unclean. Mom was going bonkers. She told my sister and me that if we got rid of Inky, she would get us new dolls. We agreed. We sold out our little friend for materialistic gain, those darn dolls. Hugging a doll isn't as satisfying as hugging a warm puppy. Poor Inky. I hope he had a good life.

Mom never left the house unless she was well dressed and had makeup on. She loved flashy but stylish clothes and wore big jewelry pieces. She worked at Cherry's, a high-quality department store in downtown New Bedford. As teenagers, my sister and I sometimes dressed almost like street urchins—drab peahens compared to my mother, the colorful peacock. We walked by the downtown stores a lot, mostly window-shopping, and stopped at Woolworths for a soda and fries at the lunch counter. We shied away from going inside Cherry's if we knew Mom was working. Although she enjoyed seeing us, Mom never thought we were dressed or made up appropriately—and she was right.

I had little regard for fashion. Mom would ask me to please wear colors other than brown and gray once in a while, and my hair was impossible to style. If I stopped by to see Mom at her work, I could count on an admonishment. I understand now that she was proud of me and wanted her coworkers to see me at my best. Unfortunately, I usually stopped by when I looked my worst. My sister visited once when Mom's boss was nearby. As my sister approached, the boss said, "What's that smell? It smells like a funeral parlor." My sister suspected it might have been her fragrance, but she kept quiet. Despite our scruffy looks and strange smells, our poor mother still loved us.

Our fragrance of choice was Shalimar, which many girls in our high schools wore. We used Noxzema skin cleaner for our faces, Pond's cold cream for moisturizing, and cherry-almond-scented Jergens lotion for our often-chapped hands. There wasn't a myriad of grooming products, as there is today.

My sister has the sweetest disposition of anyone I know. I've never known her to be moody or say an unkind word about anyone. Whenever I think of my sister, I see her smiling and hear her soft, giggly laugh. She is the sunshine to my gray. Like Mom, she always remembers to send birthday cards, and she keeps in touch with family.

Geraldine believes in giving gifts, not money, for birthdays and Christmas. She enjoys shopping and choosing things she thinks the recipient will like. She has no problem wrapping them and going to the post office, and she often adds some homemade baked goods.

Her gifts to Mom and Dad were often underappreciated. After seeing Mom wear old and torn pajamas, for one birthday, she bought her a new pair. Mom said, "Geraldine, I have a whole closet full of pajamas." And she did. Brand-new ones she hadn't worn. "Can you use them?" Mom asked my sister about the ones she had just given her. Geraldine took them back.

One year, for Dad's birthday, she made him a cake and gave him a gift certificate to his favorite restaurant. She also made him a card that referred to him as a lovable grouch. He got insulted.

One Christmas, she gave my grandmother a piece of lingerie. "Can you use it?" my grandmother asked. Geraldine took it back. Undaunted, she continued to give gifts.

Geraldine and I went to the same college, where she earned a degree in visual design. At the age of twenty, my sister was cast as leading lady in a student movie at the college and written about in the college newsletter.

> Geraldine is a vivacious person; she has that special type of charm that denotes a friendly, outgoing type of chatter. Her eyes are usually dancing with some mischievous quality while she talks.[2]

In the photo that accompanies the article, my sister reminds me of a young Diane Keaton in the movie *Reds*; her hair is pulled back in a bandana, and her eyes are soft and soulful. She looked pretty, and I was jealous. I thought she was prettier than I was.

Geraldine has always been artistic like Dad. Over the years, she has used her artistry for family gifts: a large painting for

---

[2] M. Isdepski, "On the Scene," *Southeastern Massachusetts University News*, March 30, 1967.

Mom's living room, several small paintings for me, and much-loved paintings for her young grandsons.

My sister has a love for animals, and she has always kept herself surrounded with an assortment of cats and dogs. Shadow, an Old English sheepdog, was mentioned in one of Mom's letters:

> Shadow had 14 puppies yesterday. Shadow won't go near the pups, the vet gave them bottles & formula. You should hear the racket they make. It all started when Shadow got loose one day. Geraldine doesn't know what kind of dog the father is. They all look like Shadow, or rather like Old English Sheep dogs.

Geraldine met and married Reggie, a handsome hometown boy and police officer. He had served in Vietnam with the marines. The wedding was a snazzy affair with a country club reception. She was a beautiful bride, and her long white dress was stunning. The marriage gave the world two children, Leanne and Carl, four years apart. Leanne had the Hotaling coloring: brown hair and eyes. Carl had the Norwegian looks: blond hair and blue eyes. My little sister was starting her own family, as I had. I was proud of her.

My sister kept house and lovingly raised her children. She had an extraordinary amount of patience. Her husband, despite coming from a good family and having a career in law enforcement, proved to be a scoundrel. This started to become apparent when he went missing. My sister was shocked and worried the first time he disappeared for a few days. It turned out he was a womanizer. Time and again, he cheated on my sister, often leaving home for days at a time to be with one woman or another. At first, she was patient and forgiving, but his infidelity continued, and soon we all knew about it. He had so many girlfriends Mom wondered when he had time for work. Mom wrote about X, a girlfriend he married:

X told Geraldine that Reggie had many girlfriends while he was still married to her. I guess he had one in every town. I'm surprised he ever got any work done. He owes money all over the place. X had a good offer for her car & when she told Reggie she was going to sell it, he said she couldn't because he took out a loan & he used the car for collateral. He told X that he's still paying off a loan for the roof on Geraldine's house, but Geraldine said she paid for the roof with the money she had when she married him.

The police station often called my sister to ask where he was. She usually didn't know. He just disappeared now and then. Geraldine bravely stood by him and gave him many chances. Finally, she had had enough, and they divorced after a ten-year marriage. The family felt both sadness and relief. Mom wished they had divorced sooner. She hated seeing her daughter hurt. Geraldine took a job in a bank because she needed a steady income. After the divorce, Reggie made the following comment, which Mom told me about in a letter:

When Reggie & Geraldine got divorced, he said, "Thank heavens I don't have to eat her mother's dried up chicken anymore."

This became a family joke because we all loved Mom's fried chicken. My niece, Leanne, often said in fun, "Yum. May I have more of your dried-up chicken, Nana?"

My family was strong and loyal to each other. Until I reread Mom's letters, I hadn't realized how involved my parents were with caring for my sister and her kids during the difficult times after her divorce. Dad maintained her house, which was old—built in

1844—and in need of repair. He replaced, repainted, and fixed it. Mom and Dad often helped her out around the house. Mom wrote,

> I'm so tired tonight. Your father and I went down to paint Carl's ceiling & as usual it was so bad, we had to take the whole ceiling down. What a mess! Plaster all over the place. You know what Carl's room looks like. He has things under his bed that have been missing for years. I was standing on a table and it fell apart. I opened a door and it came off its hinge. Then every time I turned around, there was a cat under my feet.

Geraldine didn't worry about clutter in the house. Far from house-proud, she was a free spirit and artist who lived in the moment and put priority on her family. On the other hand, Mom was a fanatical cleaner, and cleaning was high on her priority list. Mom complained about Geraldine not cleaning enough, and Geraldine complained that Mom was too fussy. After my sister had back surgery, Mom started cleaning her house every week. She did this for years. Geraldine told Mom she didn't have to keep cleaning, but Mom insisted. I think of Mom when I read the following from William Butler Yeats's "The Song of the Old Mother":

> I rise in the dawn, and I kneel and blow
> Till the seed of the fire flicker and glow;
> And then I must scrub and bake and sweep
> Till stars are beginning to blink and peep.

Along with doing repairs and cleaning, my parents often babysat Geraldine's two children, Leanne and Carl. They took them shopping and to the movies and had them over for dinner. Mom also took them on trips. They went to Niagara Falls and

Disney World, among other places. My parents gave Leanne and Carl some happy childhood memories they otherwise would not have had.

> I'm taking Leanne & Carl to Niagara Falls & I received the itinerary. Your father has already put a damper on it. He said he knows Leanne & Carl aren't going to have a good time. He & Nanny are so alike. To them a good time is sitting home.

Geraldine appreciated Mom's help. Mom wrote,

> In yesterday's paper they had a section where you could write something about your mother. Geraldine wrote a piece about me. It brought tears to my eyes. Here it is.

>> The time I most remember was a special one. The year was 1982 and I was a recently divorced single mother with a new job and on a very tight budget. My mother did something generous and touching. She invited me and my two young children to a week-long vacation at Disney World. We spent a wonderful week in Florida and made many happy memories. But the trip meant much more than a fun-filled vacation. It showed me how much my mother truly loved and supported me. She inspired me with a new sense of self-confidence. —Geraldine

After my sister's divorce, she dated a few characters, and my mother was suspicious of all of them.

The fellow Geraldine went out with is coming on strong. He wanted her to go out Sun. night & yesterday he came into the bank with a little stuffed ape that said, "I Love You." She said he must have told her about 15 times Sat. night how beautiful she was. She doesn't know how sincere he can possibly be.

One of the women that Geraldine works with is trying to fix her up with a fellow. He is quite young, 25. It seems he was married to a swinger and she divorced him.

After a few years of dating, my sister found love and married Richard, who worked in construction. Richard could do anything around a house. He was a talented perfectionist, so his work was always excellent. He renovated the old house and made many improvements to it. Geraldine and Richard had one child, Matthew, who was born a month premature with pneumonia. He spent the first ten days of his life in intensive care. Within days of his birth, Hurricane Gloria blew into New England, wreaking havoc, downing trees and power lines, making it hard for my sister and Richard to visit baby Matthew, who was in a children's hospital in another state. Geraldine cried when she saw him with tubes sticking out of his body, even his head. But he survived and went home after a few weeks. Geraldine and Richard have had a long, happy marriage.

My sister always remembers Mom and Dad helping her out during and after her first marriage. In later years, she wrote a Mother's Day poem that was published in the local paper:

You gave me assistance when I was ill,
And though you've grown older, you're helping
me still.

You've stood by me through good and bad,
Cheered me up when I was sad.
You've made me the person I am today.
How can I thank you? What can I say?
You are my mother, my teacher, my friend.
My gratitude to you will never end.
The nicest compliment I could get from another
Is for someone to say, "You are just like your mother."

Everything my sister and I learned about life started with our parents. We learned they weren't perfect. No one is. But they were always there for us when we needed them, and if we disappointed them at any time, they soon got over it. Geraldine and I have weathered many storms, including our divorces and the deaths of our dear parents. Now we are there for each other. We share the same memories of Mom and Dad. We are still twisted together and growing like grapevines. We are still here.

CHAPTER 5

I'm an American Girl

When I was a young lady, everyone got a new outfit for Easter. When I was twelve, I got a powder-blue dress suit. Mom and I found matching shoes, hat, gloves, and nylon stockings. I couldn't wait to wear my new outfit to Easter Sunday Mass. I would be in blue from head to toe. Dressed up that Easter Sunday, I thought I was really something special. I was starting to grow up.

Unfortunately, I was a tomboy and ripped the stockings and tore the hat before I even made it back home from church. (Once, when walking with Mom, I leapfrogged over a fire hydrant and split the skirt I was wearing right up the middle.)

Around that time, I discovered pop music and had a crush on the Everly Brothers. I loved their pitch-perfect two-part harmony as well as their handsome good looks. I knew everything that had been written about them. I owned all their albums and sang their songs. A girlfriend and I entered a talent show at the Catholic youth center to sing "Take a Message to Mary," one of their lesser-known songs from their folk album *Songs Our Daddy Taught Us*. Mom made us matching white shirts and pink skirts. Geraldine thought I did well, but I had had lots of practice and could sing either part of the harmony. Regardless, we didn't win any prize. "Let It Be Me" is still one of my favorite songs. It's haunting melody evokes my teenage years and makes me wish for romantic love.

In the 1960s, America was moving from the Eisenhower years to the Nixon years and from the war in Korea to the war in Vietnam.

When I was in my midteens, Mom and Dad built a house in a new development in the suburbs on a plot of land that was nothing but fields. Their house was the second one built on what became Temple Street. It was the last house my parents would live in and the house I would leave home from.

It was hard to leave our first house on Chestnut Street, the house of my childhood. We moved from a very old house to a brand-new one and from the city to the suburbs. I wondered what changes the new house would see for Mom and me.

When I was fifteen and a sophomore in high school, I transferred from a Catholic school to a public school. I was tired of being taught by nuns and wanted to see how things worked in the real world.

I got off to a bad start when I developed a big crush on a boy called Alfie. He had beautiful good looks. His pals were risk-takers, young guys who thought nothing of borrowing someone's car to go riding in. I often accepted a ride home from a Friday night dance in a borrowed car. I was happy to be part of Alfie's group. I had an identity and ready-made friends. The fun lessened on a night when the police followed our car for an unknown reason. We stopped the car and ran for cover in some nearby sand dunes. Hunched in the dunes and crouching down, Alfie and I saw flashlights searching for us. They didn't find us, and we thought it was a lark. But deep down, I knew we were skating on thin ice.

One of the boys in Alfie's group of friends didn't like me for some reason. He called me Fish at times to be funny. I didn't think it was funny, but I didn't challenge him. I was afraid of him because he picked on me. He stopped bothering me when he got a crush on a girl I knew. He wanted me to put in a good word for him. I said I would, but I never did.

Alfie was my first love. In my stressful world of making exceptional school grades, competing with my peers over scholarship, and struggling with religion, my heart fluttered when I saw him. I was washed with joy, and my cares and anxieties disappeared. I wanted to laugh and cry at the same time, as I was so taken by him. He became my priority.

With all the fun I was having, my grades went down. I got Bs and Cs on my report cards, and my mother didn't speak to me for weeks at a time. That hurt because I knew I had been slacking off, and I hated being estranged from Mom. Her passive-aggressive punishment—which I deserved—put a wall between us, and I needed that wall to come down. I knew I had to buckle down and pay attention to my grades. The real impetus to change came when Alfie broke up with me and gave me my first broken heart. I sat on a chair in the kitchen and gave my sob story to Mom with tears running down my face. She told me that she knew it hurt but that things would be okay (advice I now give to my grandchildren). I would go on to have several more boyfriends.

I settled down in my junior year of high school, left Alfie's group, and started studying hard to make up for lost time. I was admitted to the National Honor Society and went on to have much success in college. In time, I lost track of the good old gang. But I still remember the feelings of that first love, and I wonder what became of dear, handsome Alfie.

Whenever I am bereaved, as I was after Alfie left, I am at my most creative. I wrote lots of poems and stories in my teens. They are remarkable for their macabre elements. Consider the following opening lines to some of my poems:

> Before the conviction, Mother baked pies, washed
> clothes, kept house, and dabbled in the occult.
> Once a week, she attended Black Mass.

Lay me to rest in the earth that I love, under rock,
under sand, under sky.

I woke up dead one morning.

I feel I must tell you of the day I died.

It would matter, but it's all too late.

My works were morbid. Most were about death, damnation, ghosts, and graveyards. When I was in a better mood, I wrote about unrequited love. Consider the titles of a few poems from that time period: "The Ghost Walkers," "Letter to a Lost Soul," "Letter to a Mourner of His Child," "A Mother's Lament," and "World War III." Cheerful, right?

I wrote an unnamed piece about a woman who dreams about falling from a staircase, jumping off a boat and drowning, and almost dying in a plane crash. After waking up and discovering that she has lost both her arms and legs in a real plane crash, she says a prayer and dies. Where on earth was my mind? No doubt anxiety was at play. Not all my work was about death. I also wrote about Abraham Lincoln, the race for space, and dogs:

Mandy, my Airedale,
Who I saved from the pound,
Come lay your big brown body down
Beside me.

I never said my poems were good, only that I got creative when I was upset.

Around that time, I had an unusual problem for a person my age: I couldn't sleep. I suffered no ill effects, and I wasn't tired; I just couldn't fall asleep. Mom took me to doctors and specialists, but no cause was found, and no one could help. Perhaps my insomnia reflected a fall from grace by associating with Alfie and his friends. The insomnia lasted almost two years. At last, Mom made a novena to Saint Jude, the patron saint of lost causes, and I slept again. Either Saint Jude worked wonders, or the power of suggestion did, which could also be attributed to the saint, so I believe he did have an influence.

As long as I lived with Mom, I observed the Catholic religion; I attended weekly Mass and prayed daily. My grandmother gave me a prayer to recite on the hour: "Dear Jesus, another hour has passed; to thee I give the next and last." I became obsessed with saying the prayer during all my waking hours.

My favorite subject in high school was English literature. I fell in love with poetry and Shakespeare. Rote memorization was part of the curriculum, and I memorized many poems, which I can still recite. My favorite poem at the time was from *The Vision of Sir Launfal* by James Russell Lowell. Below is an excerpt I especially enjoyed:

> The little bird sits at his door in the sun,
> Atilt like a blossom among the leaves,
> And lets his illumined being o'errun
> With the deluge of summer it receives;
> His mate feels the eggs beneath her wings,
> And the heart in her dumb breast flutters and sings;
> He sings to the wide world, and she to her nest,
> In the nice ear of Nature which song is the best?

The last two lines are worth pondering, and I think about them every so often. Who has the better story to tell: men who go out into the world to make a living or women who stay home to care for the young? I believe both stories are inherently good and necessary.

In addition to poetry, we read plays and dissected *Hamlet* and its theme of death, which was much to my liking.

During high school, I had an odd crush on my French teacher, who was female. She wasn't physically attractive to me, but I was strangely attracted to her personality. It was the only time I was attracted to the same sex. I looked forward to French class. My crush ended when the class did.

As teenagers, we went to the park to ice-skate on the big pond at Buttonwood Park. When the water froze, signs went up that the ice was safe, and it was announced on the radio. We'd go after school, when it was already dark. There was only one light pole in the middle of the pond. We had to watch for open water since we couldn't easily see it at night. Of course, when we did see it, we had to skate right up to it through the reeds to see how dangerous it was. A few times, I broke through the ice to my knees. The ice froze in ripples, not smooth like a rink, so each skating session was a bumpy ride. But the warming house was wonderful. It had old wooden picnic tables and benches, a big roaring fire, and hot chocolate for sale. When the pond froze, it was the gathering place for teenagers.

In the summer, the hot gathering place for teenagers was the beach, and we teens argued over which beach was better, East or West. Both were in the southern end of the city, on different sides of a peninsula. I went to both but preferred West Beach because its sandy shore was farther from the sea. At East Beach, the water could get so high at high tide that it covered much of the sand. When that happened, we jumped into the water from the walled sidewalk that wrapped around the beach. Knowing the pitch of the beach, I didn't like to think how high the water was not far from the sidewalk. It was like jumping into the unknown. I was afraid of deep water.

Lying out in the sun on the sand by the water was highly therapeutic. My mind cleared, and my worries baked away. At the time, there was no knowledge of, or fear of, melanoma. Everyone I knew baked themselves silly every summer. The young girls chatted among themselves and listened to music. The boys swam, jumped, and splashed in the water.

From West Beach, we could see the fishing boats going out to sea and coming back in. I always thought about Dad when I saw a fishing boat chugging through the water.

We girls baked on the beach from June through August. Our favorite activity was "laying out"—arranging a towel on the sand and lying on it in various positions designed to produce a perfect suntan. I always had my light blue transistor radio with me—a gift for eighth-grade graduation—and occasionally a book. Books were hard to read in the bright sun, but the radio played constantly. I listened to the top forty hits on WPRO in Providence. When we girls got too hot, we went in the water. I've never known an East Coast beach not to have a rocky seabed. The endless rocks, pebbles, seaweed, sea glass, shells, and whatnot made it difficult to walk in the water, so we started swimming as soon as the water was deep enough. Many of us headed for the raft, a floating block with a diving board. I wasn't a great swimmer—I was a far better tanner—and I could barely make it to the raft without getting winded. In fact, once, I was brought back to shore by a lifeguard who saw I was getting tired. Getting to the raft was a quixotic quest, and I achieved it a few times without drowning.

One summer, Mom found me a job at an amusement part. I worked in the penny arcade from noon until ten o'clock at night, redeeming coupons won at various arcade games for prizes. I hated it since it seriously cut into my beach time. In fact, there was no beach time during the two weeks I worked. Plus, the job was boring. Most of my time was spent waiting for customers to redeem their coupons. I was bored and only half tanned. After one paycheck, Mom let me quit, and I was back to the beach, toasting to a lovely shade of brown.

Like discovering a new element, I discovered the magic of chemistry in the eleventh grade. I had little liking for it, but it was to become my life's work. Since I got good grades in it, my chemistry teacher recommended I major in it in college. I considered that. A few years later, when I applied to college, Mom and Dad encouraged me to stay in town to save money. I could go to the technical school, which happened to offer chemistry as a major. Although I would have preferred to go to a liberal arts college, I thought, *Why not?* It wasn't a hard sell because I was anxious when separated from my mother, and I could take liberal arts classes as electives.

My father paid my college tuition, even though he thought college was a waste of time for girls. He said, "You'll only get married and have kids." That turned out to be true, but having a college degree definitely helped me.

Thursday night was cruise night downtown, when teenage boys drove slowly through the streets, as in the film *American Graffiti*, checking out the girls who were walking on the sidewalks and window-shopping. My sister and I were usually among the sidewalk strollers. If we got lucky, we got a ride home with one of the boys who were cruising, all of whom we knew.

One Thursday a month was men's night at Cherry's department store, where Mom worked. Mom didn't like helping the men who came to shop.

> I have to work tomorrow, they're having "men's night." I'm not that crazy about helping men. Some of them act so stupid, they have to have a couple of drinks to get up the courage to come in the lingerie dept. & then they act so dumb.

Mom did not suffer fools gladly.

Cherry's was located in the heart of downtown. There was a bus stop right outside Cherry's front door. I knew that bus stop because it was where I had to walk if I wanted to take the bus home from my college, which was also in the downtown area.

I had two ways to get home from college: walk or walk to

the bus stop. The latter was about half the walk home, so I often walked, a distance of several miles. Sometimes when I walked home, I stopped to visit my grandmother. I visited her the day President Kennedy was killed and sat with her for a while to watch the television coverage.

If Mom saw my sister or me walking, she stopped to give us a ride. My father was another story:

> I remember your father driving past either you or Geraldine once when you were walking home from school. He never stopped to give you a ride. He just didn't think.

Getting my driver's license expanded my world significantly. But within thirty minutes of getting my license and driving Dad's car, I was stopped by the police for driving too fast in Buttonwood Park. I was going under twenty miles per hour, but that was too fast because there were small children afoot. I was let off with a warning. Later on, I got a few speeding tickets in Ohio and one in Utah. Like my father, I thought you should drive to keep up with the traffic, not the speed limit.

During my sophomore year of college, my father bought me my first car: a sea-green Volkswagen Beetle. I loved the independence that little car gave me and the long walks it saved me from. I loved driving to Cape Cod in the summer and exploring the sand dunes in Provincetown, which was still wild with nature when I visited it. I imagined I could see England from the tip of the cape. I even drove to Kingston a few times.

I excelled in college and was the only girl in the chemistry program. Getting good grades didn't come easily to me. I worked hard, often into the early morning hours, doing homework. Reports were typed, and if you made a mistake, you had to type the entire page over again. Wite-Out was in the future.

Once again, my favorite classes had to do with literature.

I took a class on Chaucer, the English poet who wrote *The Canterbury Tales*. We were graded not only on our knowledge of his writing but also on our pronunciation in reading the original Middle English of the fourteenth century. I also took a class on the dark side of American literature, featuring Edgar Allan Poe and other gloomy writers—my favorite kind. Of course I took tons of chemistry courses, which I did well in.

By the end of college, I had made the dean's list every semester, and I graduated with a 3.8 grade point average (4.0 would have meant straight As). I wasn't competing with the boys, but I was pleased when I was the only one in a class of boys-plus-me to earn an A in thermodynamics. I graduated from the University of Massachusetts summa cum laude, third in my class, with a bachelor of science degree in chemistry. I didn't realize until later what a gift my degree was to me and what a superpower chemistry was.

I was a typical American teenager. I had crushes on boys, which resulted in first happiness and then heartbreak. I rebelled against school and then grew to love learning. I loved sunbathing at the beach and ice-skating on the pond. I didn't love chemistry, but it was to enrich my life.

I didn't realize it at the time, but I was learning about my beliefs, my value system, and my personality. I was observing Mom, Dad, and my sister, tucking away what I had seen and remembering their reactions to incidents in their lives. I was a smart kid and was introspective, but I hadn't fully opened my heart to my family. As a teenager, I took them for granted. I wasn't an especially warm or chatty person. I wasn't the master of my fate. I was floating through space and time, landing wherever the winds took me.

CHAPTER 6

Family or Bust

I might have stayed in school forever, joined the hippie movement, and become a protester of the war in Vietnam. I had "Make love, not war" sentiments and was a peacenik through and through. But a different destiny awaited me—one with battles.

At the age of twenty-one, I was in my senior year of college, thinking about graduate school (I had been accepted at Brown University), when I started to feel unwell. I was dizzy and nauseated. Diagnosed with an inner ear infection, I took medication, which didn't work. I revisited the doctor and discovered that I was expecting a baby. The news was frightening in many ways. I wasn't married; I knew nothing about caring for babies; and, worst of all, I would have to tell my mother. I was sick with dread. I bit the bullet and told Mom the news.

The news broke my mother's heart, and she cried for days. I can still see her on the couch, crying and red-eyed. My father put his arm around her with a worried look on his face. I felt like an assassin, although I never had intended to hurt anyone. It was the only time I saw Mom and Dad hold each other, and it was in grief brought about by my misadventure. After she stopped crying, Mom stopped talking to me. She had no words for the situation. When I fainted during a blood check, Mom started to forgive me. She was still my mother and hated to see me unwell. So we resumed talking but not about the baby.

When I was twenty-one, I met nineteen-year-old Kent, the father of my unexpected child, while working at a men's clothing store during college. The store was one big room in a concrete building lit by rows of fluorescent lights and filled with suits, jackets, trousers, and other items of men's clothing. The store had a tailoring station and a small ladies' clothing area. I worked as a cashier in the small open office near the double-glass-door entrance, the only place where the sun shone in. I would hear the sound of Kent's motor scooter come into the parking lot and would perk up. Kent was always cheery. When he came through the entry doors, his smile made the already-well-lit room, along with my disposition, brighter. Kent was nice looking and clean cut. With his crew cut, he looked like an army recruit, and he stood tall and straight, with no typical teenage slouching.

Mom insisted I work during college, although all I wanted to do was study and get good grades. (Years later, she wondered what my life would have been like had she not insisted on my working.) At work, Kent stocked merchandise and helped bag sales in an area near the cashier. Suits were carefully folded and boxed. He was a Catholic boy who was studying textile engineering at the same college where I was studying chemistry. We struck up a friendship and went on a few dates.

We had actually quit dating by the time I found out a baby was on the way. We talked about the situation and agreed to marry. Although we were both young, Kent was quick to believe that marriage was the best solution. Abortion was never an option. Fortunately, I could finish college because I would graduate three months before the baby's birth. With a solution in place, I told my mother, completely devastating her. I'm not sure what upset her more, the baby or the fact that I would marry and leave home. I remembered that she hadn't wanted children. Had she expected me not to have any? Was I expected not to leave home? Thankfully, my sister was delighted with the news of our baby. Kent's parents were friendly and reassuring from the start. They weren't filled with anxiety, as Mom was.

Kent and I chose to be a family. We didn't have a love match or even similar personalities, although we both loved our unborn daughter. We hadn't known each other long enough to know if we were compatible. We were married in the Holy Name Catholic Church on an unfortunate but convenient date, April 1, the start of our spring break from college. The redbrick church had cathedral ceilings and an ornate marble altar, like many Catholic churches built in the nineteenth century. I wore a white brocade coat-and-dress ensemble, a short veil, and cat-eye glasses. We exchanged vows in soft, nervous voices. In our wedding pictures, we look pleasant but serious. At a local restaurant, my parents hosted a luncheon for about fifty relatives and friends. Afterward, Kent and I vacationed for few days in Laconia Notch in the rugged White Mountains of New Hampshire. The scenery was lovely, but I came down with a bad sore throat and didn't feel well the whole time. When we visited the Old Man in the Mountain, a rock formation that resembled an old man's face, we didn't know that in time, it would crumble and fall apart like our marriage.

I changed my last name to Kent's, although my college adviser recommended not changing it. He said that some professional women continued to use their maiden names when they married. I wish I had taken his advice, but at the time, I believed that almost all women took their husbands' last names. It was the socially acceptable convention. So was promising to love, honor, and obey. I was so relieved to marry and heal Mom's broken heart that I didn't stop to think of the independence I would be losing or the sacrifices I would make. My name was only the first loss.

I had no preparation for having a baby. There wasn't much help for new mothers in the 1960s. The book *What to Expect When*

You're Expecting wasn't published until 1984. No hospital training classes were offered, and my mother didn't speak of the baby for the nine months of my pregnancy. I was alone and frightened on the precipice of something life-changing. But I knew it would do no good to complain. I had cast my lot in with motherhood, and it was time to accept what fate had intended for me.

For the first few months of my pregnancy, nausea persisted, and I couldn't eat certain things I loved, such as chocolate. It left a sick taste in my mouth. Inexplicably, my face broke out in a horrible case of acne, which I never had had as a teenager. Those discomforts and mutilations disappeared around the time I felt the baby move. At first, it was a gentle flutter, like a baby bird attempting an inaugural flight. Later on, arms, legs, and heaven knows what else kicked and poked about like the alien in John Hurt's compromised body in the movie *Alien*. All I knew about labor was that the pains were said to be like menstrual cramps.

After a bumpy start, I had an easy second half of pregnancy. I graduated college when I was six months along, and I gained only ten pounds total. I was working at the clothing store when I went into labor. "I'm off! See you later!" I chirped to my coworkers, having no idea what was ahead of me.

Around two o'clock in the morning, I thought the cramping was bad enough to go to the hospital. After admission, I was given drugs to induce twilight sleep, probably morphine and scopolamine. No one at the hospital told me what to expect. I slipped into a state of semiconsciousness and later remembered a few things, including pain that seemed to last for years. The twilight-sleep drugs caused short-term amnesia, and I lost my sense of time. At one point, I heard someone screaming from a distance and thought it might be me. Kent was ushered to a waiting area—I would next see him after the baby was born—and I was left alone in a bed with side rails that restricted my movement.

Education and breathing exercises can help some women prepare for childbirth. I had neither. I was drugged, ignorant, and terrified. Mom had ropes to pull on when I was born, and I had drugs that caused delirium. The pain was like nothing I had ever experienced, and only a woman can understand it. The pain ebbs and flows, unless you are in a twilight sleep, when time is out of focus. Then the pain seems to last forever. Not every labor is like this. Some women experience short labors and relatively little pain, as I did with my second baby.

After about ten hours, my baby was born, and the pain stopped. My daughter Lisa was born on a late-summer Sunday in early September, Labor Day weekend. (As a popular rhyme says "Sunday's child is fair and wise and good and gay.") Kent and I had created a new human being.

Seeing your baby for the first time is an almost otherworldly experience. You wonder how two ordinary people could have brought this extraordinary little being into the world.

That evening, the first time I saw my mother after I became a mother myself, she was radiant. "Oh, Kath, she looks just like you. She's beautiful!" she said. I knew then that my sin of an unplanned pregnancy was forgiven. I had my child, and she was welcomed into the family. Mom was ready to embrace her grandchild and move on.

When Mom became a grandmother, we started calling her Nana. I am also Nana to my grandchildren.

Lisa was a fretful baby, no doubt because I was a fretful mother who herself had had a fretful mother. Mom helped me with her, and together we taught her all kinds of bad habits. For example, she had to be sung to and rocked to sleep each night. Mom started doing that, and I assumed it was the right thing to do. Baby Lisa loved "The Banana Boat Song." Mom and I sang that song until we went hoarse. If Lisa woke up during the night, which she did often, I would walk with her nestled on my shoulder and sing to her until she fell back to sleep. I would put her back in her crib in slow motion so I didn't wake her. While keeping my eyes on her, I would then crawl on all fours to the door so she didn't see me. If one of my knees hit a squeaky floorboard, she woke up, and the singing and walking started again. The worst times were when she cried and I couldn't figure out what was wrong. As a scientist, I looked for a reason, but as a mother, I learned that sometimes babies cry for no reason at all. Maybe they are so new they just want to hear what crying sounds like.

Kent and I lived in public housing while he completed college, not far from Mom and Dad. Our housing was essentially a downscaled condo. It had the requisite features but no frills; we could see the pipes under the sinks and hear every word spoken by the next-door neighbors. No doubt they could hear me too as I sang along to my favorite albums. Judy Collins was my idol at the time, and I sang her plaintive songs along with her. "Send in the Clowns" still moves me. I identified with it. I was a clown; I had a good sense of humor, and I sometimes did stupid things.

Two years later, after Kent's graduation from college, I moved six hundred miles to Ohio for Kent's job. We were reluctant to leave New Bedford, but his degree in textile technology suited specific companies, none of which were local. Our meager belongings were put in a moving van, and Kent drove the family car. Mom and I boarded a plane, along with my active two-year-old. We were moving away from public housing into a brand-new townhouse, away from childhood into maturity.

Lisa, as a toddler, had masses of curly blonde hair, brown eyes, and a sunny disposition. Mom flew to Ohio with me and stayed for two weeks, cleaning the new townhouse we had rented and helping me to get adjusted. The flight was terrible for two reasons: I was leaving home after living for twenty-two years under my father's roof, and to top it off, the plane got in a holding pattern over Connecticut for two hours. We made the connecting flight in New York City by only minutes.

Saying goodbye to Mom when she left Ohio was as difficult a thing as I had done up until that time. We both cried and cried.

After that first visit, she visited a couple of times a year, and I did the same, gritting my teeth every time I got on a plane. (After the Piper Cub flight, I developed a fear of flying.) We talked on the phone every Sunday. It was then that she began to write her weekly letters. Those precious letters.

Although I missed my mother terribly, I discovered that I had to live apart from her to gain my independence. Every time I was in New Bedford, I was her little girl again. As a mother, I had to be independent and strong for my own children.

Kent was a terrific father, but his job required him to travel a lot. I was alone with Lisa much of the time. My early marriage years were a lonely time for me. I had been uprooted from my home and left alone with a toddler. When I look back, I see how this was similar to my mother's situation. She had married my father after knowing him for only a month, moved away from her childhood home, and been alone with me while he went fishing.

Kent and I had lived in Ohio for two months, when we had to take Lisa to the emergency room. She had walked into the street outside our town house, and Kent had spanked her bottom to teach her not to walk into traffic. Crying, she stumbled her way to me and fell on a concrete step, which split her forehead open to the bone. A kindly neighbor drove us to Children's Hospital, where they patched her up. I could hear her crying behind a door, and then the crying stopped. *My God, she's died*, I thought. Fortunately, she had just fallen asleep. Since she had a head injury, I was advised to wake her up at night to make sure she was conscious. That was yet another in a long line of sleepless nights with many rounds of "The Banana Boat Song."

Kent and I didn't want Lisa to be an only child, so we planned to have another. But nothing happened. I got pregnant with Lisa without even knowing it, yet we couldn't make another baby. After visiting a specialist and taking fertility pills, I got pregnant for a second time four years after my first child and two years after we started trying.

My second daughter was born on a blistering-hot Tuesday in early June. ("Tuesday's child is full of grace.") My mother and her mother, Nan, traveled to Ohio to help me. That turned out to be the last time I saw my grandmother. I picked them up at the bus terminal in the morning and then went to the hospital and delivered baby Tracey in the afternoon. Her birth was much easier and quicker. I discovered that with the first baby, you get to the hospital as soon as possible; with the second, you delay as long as possible. I arrived at the hospital at two o'clock, and she was born two hours later. The nurses explained everything that was happening. It was a completely different experience for me. I was educated and unafraid.

Mom and Nan stayed for two weeks. Blonde, blue-eyed Tracey was an easy baby. She seldom fussed, and she slept well with no rocking and singing. I put her in her crib, and she fell asleep—like magic.

I think Tracey might have been one of the last babies in Ohio to wear cloth diapers and drink formula that had been sterilized in bottles. Before she was a year old, no-pin Pampers were on the market, disposable Playtex nursers were readily available, and Similac could be bought in a can. These were godsends for busy mothers.

After Tracey was born, I put away Judy Collins and sang along to John Denver. He and I were both twenty-seven when he recorded *Rocky Mountain High*. I was lucky enough to see John in live performances twice in his short life. He resonated with me. I cared for the environment, as he did, and we seemed to share other values.

When Tracey was two months old, Kent and I drove the six hundred miles back to my parents' house in an old Buick station wagon. We had our two children and an active wire-haired terrier with us. In New York City, we ran into a traffic nightmare that tested our parenting skills. Two oil trucks had collided and spilled oil on the road. Traffic was stopped for the cleanup. It was another hot summer day. We sat in the car for two hours in ninety-degree heat. Tracey cried for her formula, which had spoiled, and the dog cried for water, which had run out. I was starting to get frightened, but thankfully, traffic started to move again, and we stopped at the first rest stop we saw. We survived but with frazzled nerves.

During that summer visit, the dog chewed the woodwork in my parents' downstairs den. They never repaired it, so it was always a reminder of that trip, and a few years later, when the dog ran away and was never found, the damaged woodwork reminded me of my lost dog.

Another trip took us to my parents' house for Christmas. Getting there was uneventful and took the usual fourteen hours (the speed limit hadn't been changed from seventy to fifty-five miles per hour yet, so we could make good time). On the way home to Ohio, we ran into a blizzard, and the drive took twenty-four hours. My mother was worried when I didn't call after the usual amount of time the trip took, but there was nothing I could do. Mobile phones weren't around yet. The snow was so deep we couldn't pull off the highway to look for a pay phone, so we just kept pushing on.

The more we traveled to my parents' house with the kids, the better prepared for travel we became. We packed plenty of food, water, and other supplies. Despite the inconvenience of travel, the trips were good for the kids. They got to visit their two sets of grandparents; they explored New Bedford, the great whaling town; and they developed a lifelong love of the seashore and beaches. We visited New Bedford for two weeks every summer, but the blizzard year was our last Christmas visit.

Kent and I bought our first house together shortly before Tracey was born. It was a small cottage in a family community and cost $19,000. We had never taken on a debt of such magnitude and were terrified, but we needed room for two children. Kent repainted every room, and we fixed up the nursery. We were happy to bring Tracey home to our own house.

Lisa loved her little sister; Kent and I loved them both; and for a while, we had a happy little family. As the oldest child, Lisa taught Kent and me how to be parents. Every first for her was a first for us too. Lisa was a pleasant and healthy child. She gave us one scare when she was five years old and had double pneumonia with a fever of 105 degrees. The pneumonia weakened her lungs, and for a while, she had frequent respiratory problems, which she grew out of. I was a stay-at-home mom until she went to school. By then, I had learned that kids can survive injuries and illnesses. Tracey was a happy toddler who walked when she was nine months old; she was self-assured and ahead of all typical baby developments.

Mom visited us once or twice a year. As usual, she and I both cried when she left. Her letters captured her emotions:

> It was fun to walk to school and pick Lisa up at noontime. Of course I always get very weepy when it's time to leave.

> I had a nice time in Ohio, it's hard to leave 'tho, once I get there I have to think about leaving again. I wish I didn't blubber so much. When I go aboard the plane my mascara is running down my cheeks & I always look like a wreck.

As they grew up, my two daughters were added to the list of family members Mom corresponded with. As the kids learned to read, she printed their letters by hand. Her letters to the kids were short and described something she thought they'd like to hear about. Often, she enclosed little trinkets. These trinkets are still found occasionally in an old box or closet, and they trigger happy memories of young children and mothers.

When Lisa was in sixth grade, her school had a gymnastics competition. By coincidence, she had been taking gymnastics lessons and was quite good. In the competition, she won gold medals for balance beam and all-around. I was so happy you would have thought she'd won an Olympic medal. Mom wrote to Lisa,

> I sure wish I could have been out there to see you win the gold medal. Too bad we couldn't all live around each other like we did when I was growing up. When I stop to think of it, we didn't even have a car. The first car my father had was when your Mom was a baby. I can't understand how we could get along without a car, but everyone lived close by & I guess we didn't get out of the neighborhood too often.

While Lisa was in school, a friend and I often took our younger children to the park for outings in the fresh air. Afterward, we shared a few glasses of wine at her house. That was the start of my troublesome relationship with alcohol. I was lonely due to Kent's traveling, and those glasses of wine tasted good.

I once lost Tracey when she was a toddler. Mom wrote in one letter,

> Did you watch that movie on TV last night, *Adam*? All I could think of was Tray. He was lost in a Sears store in the mall, but he was found dead. Thank heavens Tray's story had a happy ending.

I had taken Tracey shopping with me at a large indoor mall, the kind they were building in the 1970s, with big anchor stores at the ends and dozens of boutiques in between. We stopped to browse in a B. Dalton bookstore. After finding some books I liked, I stood in line to pay for them. Tracey was standing by my side, wearing a light purple snowsuit. When I looked down, all I saw was a mass of platinum-blonde hair. At some point, I glanced down and noticed she was gone. Since I didn't want to lose my place in line, I assumed she had wandered off to see a book and would be back in a minute. Not looking for her immediately was one of my worst mistakes as a mother. I let her down because I didn't want to lose my place in line.

After she didn't return in a few minutes, I left the line and started looking for her. My quiet calls to her quickly became shouts, and I was escorted to the mall office in tears, where the management had me sit down to regain composure. I was frantic and scared to death—I had lost my baby! Can you imagine what it's like to hear your child's description broadcast over the mall's PA system? Every mother fears the worst. I thought I would never see that little toddler in her purple snowsuit again. I wondered, *How will I tell Kent I lost Tracey? What will this do to my mother?* I considered Tracey might have left the mall, since the bookstore was next to a main door, or she might have been abducted. I was sick with worry.

After two of the worst hours of my life, she was found by a clerk in a Sears store not far from the bookstore. Tracey had wandered into the toy department and had been happily browsing the toys. I hurried home and got there before Kent arrived home from work. By that time, the story, with its happy outcome, was safe to tell. I didn't consider not telling him. I was, and still am, honest and open.

After several years of marriage to Kent, the differences in our personalities started to surface. Kent was a good person and a great father, and he maintained the house, as did most men of the time. Men were expected to take charge of the finances and make significant family decisions. Wives were expected to take care of the children and perform household chores. The boundaries were clear. Unfortunately, I was hopeless at household skills, such as cooking and sewing. They didn't interest me. I was a scholar. I had been an A student, well respected, and accepted into a graduate program. Occasionally, Kent questioned my abilities. "Why can't you do this?" he would ask when I couldn't make a decent salad. (I cut the lettuce pieces too big.) I thought, *What about my A in thermodynamics, Kent?* Things might have been better between us if I had tried to be a better homemaker.

Like my mother before me, I had chosen a wonderful person but an ill-suited partner. Stressors, such as being pregnant, can lead to unfortunate life choices. Mom married Dad because there was a chance he would see combat during World War II. I married Kent because I was going to have a baby, which incidentally got him out of the draft for the Vietnam War.

In time, my self-esteem took a beating. I went from being defined by my scholarship to being defined as a wife, which I wasn't good at. In the end, I had little sense of self. I started to pipe-dream that Kent would magically exit my life. At that point, I decided things had to change, since wishing my life away was no way to live. I had to get myself—and him—into a better place. I had to know who I was, and I needed to make my own decisions. While under Kent's roof, that wasn't going to happen.

When Mom came to visit, she noticed we were having problems:

> I hated to see you & Kent arguing when I was out there. I hope things are OK.

After many arguments, Kent and I agreed to end the marriage. We had been married for seven years. We had married young, he traveled a lot for his job, and we never really got to know each other. We were frustrated and angry and, by that point, had no interest in working things out. The kids were becoming anxious about our arguments. The situation had to change.

Luckily, Ohio had passed a no-fault divorce law, and to divorce, you didn't have to do horrible things, such as blame each other for some infraction and call witnesses to support your claims. You agreed there was no blame that the marriage didn't work. On the first day the law was enacted, we drove together to the court. We went before a judge and answered just a few questions. We said the marriage wasn't working and agreed it should end. The court was busy, and since the no-fault divorce was new, they kept proceedings to a minimum. The court hearing took five minutes. It took longer to find a parking space.

Afterward, Kent and I had lunch. It was the best lunch we ever had, because we felt relieved and because I hadn't cooked it. I got custody of the kids and responsibilities for the house. Kent paid me ten dollars per week per child—the minimum amount by law—for their support. It was a small amount, but I knew I would manage. Shortly before the divorce had become official, I had started a full-time job. I asked nothing from my parents, only acceptance.

I was the first person in my extended family to get a divorce. Mom blamed me for it. In fact, I *was* the one who'd initiated proceedings, but I'd recognized that the situation had to change, and I'd known Kent was unlikely to be the initiator. He might have been unhappy, but he wasn't as miserable as I was—alone and raising two young children.

I wanted to return to using my maiden name, but my divorce attorney, like my college adviser before him, advised against a name change, so I wouldn't have a last name different from the kids'. I kept my ex-husband's name.

I needed a new car to get to my new job. The old Buick station wagon was on its last legs. I asked Dad if he would loan me the money. He wouldn't. So I bravely took out a bank loan and ordered a new Pontiac Ventura in fire-engine red. When the car arrived, I hopped into it and drove home only to discover that it had been made wrong. It had a bench seat in the front and a center console. What the heck? I had ordered bucket seats. In my enthusiasm to pick up the car, I had failed to notice the problem. Embarrassed, I took the car back to the dealer. They offered me $500 to keep it. Out of shame, I accepted. This illustrates the low self-esteem

I had at the time. I hadn't made the mistake or delivered the car. The blame was on the Pontiac dealer, but I assumed it and drove that ugly car for years. It was reliable but a constant reminder of what I thought of as my stupidity. But it was also a symbol of one of my first steps toward establishing my own identity.

In that ugly car, my kids and I took the road trip of our lives. When they were ten and six years old, the kids and I packed a Coleman cooler full of milk and sandwiches, tossed Doritos and Coke into the backseat, and headed west. Our destination was Salt Lake City, Utah, where my cousin lived with her husband. My mom would meet us there; she was flying out. I made good time, driving eight hundred miles per day. I knew I would never again have the endurance, or fearlessness, for another trip like this. This was newfound bravery. I was growing.

We arrived safely in Salt Lake City. Once there, we reunited with Mom and decided to drive south to the Grand Canyon and then on to Las Vegas. On the map, it looked like a fairly short drive, so off we went. Mom, the kids, and I spent the night at a motel in St. George, Utah, halfway to Vegas, and left for the Grand Canyon the next morning.

The vistas of the American West are otherworldly. Photos don't capture the natural beauty of this land; it has to be seen to be fully appreciated. The rock formations, terra-cotta mesas, buttes, valleys, canyons, and desert formations were like nothing I had ever seen. They were awesome. Even the absence of green grass was startling.

Kanab, Utah, is a town I'll never forget. Driving through it, I heard police sirens coming up behind me and looked in the rearview mirror. The police were after me; they motioned for me to pull over. I was in shock; I didn't know what law I had broken. I was cited for speeding. I hadn't seen the speed-limit sign because a panel truck had been parked in front of it; when the police pointed to the sign, the truck was gone, and I saw that I had been going over the limit.

Mom was crying along with the kids. Since I had heard horror stories of small-town justice, I wanted to get out of that mess quickly. The police instructed me to follow them to the judge's house. When we arrived, the judge was awakened from his nap, and he proceeded to read me my rights. Good grief. Was I under arrest? Could I be thrown in jail? I asked the judge, "What happens if I plead guilty?"

He said, "You'll pay a twenty-dollar fine."

I opened my wallet, paid the fine, and was out of there. I had saved the day. Mom stopped crying, and we went on to have our adventure at the Grand Canyon.

Thanks in part to the visit with the judge, it took more than eight hours to drive the two hundred miles from St. George, Utah, to the North Rim of the Grand Canyon. The canyon is spectacular, a wonder of nature, but we had no time to linger. By the time we arrived, it was already getting dark, and we had to get back to our motel.

On the trip back, driving through the desert, we saw only a single sign of life: another moving car. Nothing else, not even a cow. I stayed close to that car, tailgating, and probably scared the life out of the driver. For hours, we drove through the desert in pitch blackness, except for my headlights, and there was still no sign of St. George, our destination. Everyone in the car was anxious. I was concerned that our fuel would run out or that I was driving in the wrong direction. Finally, coming over a hill, we saw city lights and knew we had made it back to civilization and our beds for the night.

The next morning, we traveled on to Las Vegas, where the temperature was 108 degrees Fahrenheit. We spent the day in a few air-conditioned casinos, including Circus Circus for the kids; had some good food; and then began the drive back to Salt Lake City, once again in blackness but with no panic this time. We were seasoned. Mom flew home, and I packed the kids into the car for our return trip.

On the return drive to Ohio, the kids and I drove through the Rocky Mountains and high-elevation pine trees. After crossing the Rockies, I had planned to stop on the east side of Denver. That turned out to be a mistake because the land was desolate between Denver and Kansas City. I expected to find a motel around seven o'clock. I found several motels, but all were filled to capacity. In desperation, I pulled into a little park and tried to bunker down with the kids. We couldn't sleep, so I continued driving to find a motel that had vacancies. Finally, around midnight, I found a sleazy motel. Being desperate, I rented a room that was noisy from what seemed like hourly traffic in the room next door. The noise and activity unsettled me.

At four o'clock in the morning, I woke the kids, and we left. Being up so early, we had a great view of the Perseid meteor shower, a splendid sight and a redeeming outcome from the motel snafu. Seeing the dawn sky was like seeing the doors to heaven. God was right behind them. I never took a long road trip again, but my children and I have memories to last a lifetime from that trip out west. I congratulated myself on a job well done.

The postdivorce years went better for everyone at first. My older daughter, Lisa, sailed through her school years with few problems. She got good grades and associated with good kids. To my knowledge, she didn't smoke, drink, or use drugs. She grew up with the common sense that I lacked. Lisa was Mom's first grandchild, and Mom loved her. Among other things, Mom taught her manners about correspondence, about replying to letters and writing thank-you notes. Leave it to Mom to teach those niceties. Mom always wrote thank-you notes for anything she received. The following are from letters to me:

> Thanks a lot for your birthday card & gifts. Your father & I were both born on a Tue. & so were you, 5:10 PM.

Received your anniversary card. Thank you. Your
father & I both forgot about our anniversary.

In general, Mom's teaching methods were direct, and she
looked for outcome. I taught by example. Since my children
were well mannered and well behaved, my mothering skills were
working.

I read to Lisa and Tracey every night when they were
children, but I failed to pass along my love of reading. They were
both interested in more active pursuits: sports, concerts, roller-
skating, and the like. I wonder why neither of them inherited
the reading gene.

My younger daughter, Tracey, who had been a great baby,
began to rebel at the age of twelve. I should have seen it coming.
A few years earlier, she had drawn up a contract for me to sign.
She had ten demands, and I was to select five of them that I agreed
to. These were some of her demands:

- I will not call Tracey a veggie name, such as sweet potato,
  or sweetheart or little angel.
- I will let her go to the roller rink until at least 10:00 p.m.
- I will let Tracey like any boy she wants, because she has
  good judgment, and it's her life.
- I will not expect her to do all the things I did in fifth
  grade.

This my favorite:

- I will let Tracey get drunk or have one can of beer over
  two days.

She added, "I'll probably never do this, so pick it." I didn't
dare take the chance.

At the end of the contract, she gave me her Christmas list. I was to sign it without comment. I signed with the comment "I agree to part but not all. I'm still the boss." I hadn't realized things had been so unsettling for her. Kids in Middle America were growing up faster than I had.

Tracey became a teenage rebel, much as I had been and much as teenagers will probably be in the future. Her friends in junior high school were adventurous risk-takers who sometimes got into trouble.

During that time, Tracey was habitually late for school, despite my efforts to wake her before I left for work. I was warned by the school about her tardiness. I made sure she was physically out of bed before I left the house. Even then, she was late. Finally, the school authorities threatened me with jail time for child neglect. The threat had the desired effect, and Tracey started showing up to school on time. Those were hard times for both Tracey and me. Some of our hardest.

One day she and Lisa asked me which of them I liked best. I truly had no favorite. My girls were unique, and I loved them equally. I said that while I loved them both the same, Tracey needed more attention at the time. My older daughter, Lisa, wise and patient, understood.

In the state of Ohio, a twelve-year-old child of divorce could decide which parent to live with. When Tracey turned twelve, Kent asked her to live with him in South Carolina, where he had relocated with his second wife and her children. I believed that a girl needed to be raised by her birth mother, especially as she was entering her teenage years. Unavoidably, in this Sophie's-choice situation in which Tracey had to decide which parent to live with, a heart would be broken. Tracey chose to remain with me, breaking not my heart but her father's. In truth, I would have done anything to keep her with me. But it didn't come to that. I am thankful Kent didn't bring the matter to court, but I'm sorry his heart was broken. He loved Tracey as much as I did.

Thankfully, Tracey made new friends. One girl, Becky,

became her lifelong best friend. They played softball, and their coach was one tough cookie. He treated his team of girls as if they were in boot camp. That approach was good for my daughter, who needed a firm hand and clear directions. Tracey excelled at softball, and under Becky's influence, her behavior changed for the better. Like me, Tracey had gotten in with the wrong crowd. Once out of it, she did well in school and focused her attention on sports and other healthy activities. Thank God for good friends. Tracey's teenage rebellion showed me how easily we change under an influence.

While married to Kent, I went to Bible studies at the Catholic church we attended. I found the Bible history classes especially interesting; plus, they got me out of the house for a while. During one of those classes, I met the instructor, a Catholic priest, who had a profound impact on my life. I will call him David to protect his privacy. He was a good man, a holy man.

As I came to know that my marriage was unsalvageable, I approached David about marriage counseling. I learned that I needed to work on my self-esteem. If I could love myself and be happy, I could then be a more giving person to others.

After my divorce, life resumed some level of a new normalcy, but taking care of two young children, working full-time, and maintaining a house tired me out. I was often lonely. However, if I thought the hardest parts were over, I was in for some startling surprises. They were yet to come. But as always, my mother was there for me, comforting, counseling, and providing company.

CHAPTER 7

——⁂——

Love Sure Is Weird

I suspect my family is similar to other families. Occasionally, love or a relationship trips us up and makes seemingly normal people do weird things.

Consider my mom and dad. In 1994, they had been married for fifty years. We celebrated their anniversary at a quaint restaurant nestled among trees on a wooded country road. Geraldine and I picked up the tab. My parents had paid for every meal we'd ever had with them, and we owed them more than we could ever repay. They were extraordinarily generous to Geraldine and me.

Unfortunately, I can't say Mom and Dad had a happy marriage. When a friend commented on their anniversary, Mom wrote the following:

> My friend said, "You must have a great marriage for it to have lasted 50 years." I said "It's been 50 years of HELL!"

Two years earlier, she had written,

Looking at the date reminded me, today Dad & I have been married 48 yrs. It's hard to believe we haven't killed each other by now, we never agree on anything, but we're hanging in there.

Mom and Dad turned out to be a mismatched couple. He was an old-school Norwegian, a commercial fisherman, and she was a modern American girl who had wanted to become a movie star. They disagreed on virtually everything, even news from far-off shores like Ireland. Mom wrote,

What do you think of Bobby Sands? I wish I had just a little bit of his will power. Your father and I are on opposite sides. I feel in a way he was a martyr but your father thinks he was a kook. Whatever, he didn't have an easy death and so young!

Early in their marriage, since he spent most of his time at sea, my father wanted to stay home when his boat came in. My mother, alone most of the time with my young sister and me, wanted to go out. Mom and Dad usually ended up staying home since Mom was too tired to argue. She was busy feeding us, keeping us clean, and entertaining us. As young children, we never had family adventures, only outings with Mom.

While home, Mom tended to the house and yard, and she wanted to explore the world; when he was home from fishing, Dad wanted to relax. He had seen enough of the world at sea. They had few interests in common, not even religion. Dad was a nonpracticing Protestant who didn't believe in an afterlife. Mom, a Catholic, believed not only in heaven but also that she should be made a saint for living with Dad.

Mom loved to travel, but my father didn't. They visited Hawaii but discovered they hated the place. Mom said it was "hot and buggy," and Dad said he had seen enough water for a lifetime.

Since neither enjoyed the water, I asked my mother why they'd chosen to visit Hawaii. She said that at that time, it was the place to go, and all the neighbors were going. They wanted to see what all the fuss was about. To them, Hawaii was much ado about nothing. Here's a glimpse of their adventure, as found in one of Mom's letters:

> Our hotel room is air conditioned. As a matter of fact it's almost too cold and we have it set on low. Your father and I are at odds about it most of the time. I turn it off for an hour or two, then he turns it back on. We went to a German restaurant that was in the shopping area, so your father and I went shopping & that was a big mistake. He got very cranky and wouldn't go in any of the stores … one had aloha socks that your father had seen advertised, but when I called him into the store he wouldn't come. Now today he said just because he didn't go in was no reason not to buy him any socks.

Dad and Mom went to Norway to visit his homeland. It was his only visit home, and for once, he and Mom had a good time. Mom sent a cheerful letter to me:

> It seems like we've been in Norway forever. I *love* it over here. I think if you and Geraldine were here I would stay forever. Everything is very modern and clean. As I sit here I'm facing a big rock mountain. Across the street, a few sheep are running around. I wish Lee & Tray could see all of this & all the wide open spaces. They would love it, I think.

They talked about going to Alaska but never made it. They were getting older and weren't up for the adventure.

After Dad retired, Mom loved going on day trips. The trips filled her days and got her out of the house. Sometimes she went with my sister, but usually, she went with one of the girls she worked with at Cherry's or her hairdresser, Jane. As they aged, Cherry's girls relied on Jane to drive, especially at night. Jane was the only one who could still see. Mom's letters are peppered with stories of her adventures:

> I went to see *La Cage Aux Folles*. It started at 7 and got out at 11. It was a very funny movie, made in France with English subtitles. Your father had a fit because I was out so long. He's been talking about it every day. Last night when we pulled in the driveway he said, "Shall I put the car away or are you going out?" He forgets all the times he was out getting bombed while I was home. He doesn't know it yet but I'm going to see *The Mikado* Saturday night.

This letter is about a trip with my sister and her young son Matthew:

> 'Tho the weather was brutal, we went on that trip. Your father drove me to Fairhaven, complaining all the way about how foolish we were to go. There were 2 buses & they were both full, so if we were foolish we weren't alone. Our first stop in Newport was a tour of the Beechwood House. They had all the attendants dressed in costume and they tried to include the kids in the conversation. Matthew was bored & would have no part of it. When the

tour finished, we got back on the bus & drove to the beach. The surf was unbelievable, rough but beautiful. They had a kite-flying contest & most of the kites blew apart it was so windy. After a box lunch we went to Belmont Castle. Matthew again was bored. They had a sword fight & got the kids into the action, but Matthew wouldn't do anything. Later we had cake & juice & a magic show with a fire-eater & he enjoyed that. It was a very nice day, well worth the cost.

My father ridiculed my mother because she liked to go on day trips. Regardless, she still went places because she couldn't sit at home like he did. Mom learned to survive, and their marriage lasted. Dad cramped her style, but she carried on. That was the nature of their love, and it sure was weird. Mom wrote,

I had a beautiful day yesterday. The weather was fine & the trip *[to Boston]* was great. Your father complained all the while he was driving me to the bus. He doesn't want to go, but he resents it when I go. Any way I had a good time in spite of him. We ate at Victoria Station, it was an old railroad car restaurant on the Charles River. The food was very good. The play was at the Park Plaza, a real elegant hotel. The play was downstairs & it was cabaret style. Before it started, a waiter and waitress brought a birthday cake to our table & started to sing Happy Birthday to me. When I told them it wasn't my birthday they got into a big fight. It was all part of the act & the start of the play. The play had all songs from Broadway & it was one of the best I've ever seen. I'm so glad I went.

Dad said he built the house on Temple Street so he could enjoy it. Why would he want to go out? Being a homebody myself, I understood his way of thinking. But I applauded my mother for being true to herself. I loved reading her letters wherein she described a happy time she'd had. Mom went to the Christmas show at Radio City, the casinos in Atlantic City, and other events in all the states surrounding Massachusetts. I went on one trip with her to the Hyannis Playhouse on Cape Cod, where we saw *Evita*. My aunt Tillie went too. It was October and quite cold. After being served lunch by the cast, we enjoyed the show. I liked the music so much I bought the soundtrack and played it constantly on my drive home to Ohio. Whenever I hear Evita singing at the Casa Rosada, I think of that trip to the playhouse. There must have been a little magic in that cold air for me to have such rich memories of it.

My father hated those day trips, but he also hated my mother going on them without him, so occasionally, always reluctantly, he accompanied her. They once went on a bus tour to Gillette Castle.

> Your father and I are taking a little trip on Sat. We're going on a tour to Conn. When I took Carl on the whale watch, he said I never ask him to go any place. I shoved the paper under his nose & said "pick a place." He picked the Gillette Castle. It's a riverboat cruise, a meal, and a tour of the castle. Of course now he's sorry he said he would go. He would rather stay home.

At the castle, the tour guide asked my father how he pronounced his name, Knut. He said, "Cah-nute," and she said, "Oh, you pronounce the *K*!"

My father said, "That's what it's there for." He could be pretty sarcastic.

Mom could be sarcastic too:

> Your father said his hands were cold & I offered
> to let him wash the pots & pans in some nice hot
> dishwater, but he didn't buy that.

In retirement, Dad was very inactive. He and Mom lived in their beautiful modern house on Temple Street. His recliner was situated in the living room, by a window in a prime location for reading and watching TV. When he smoked, a tall metal ashtray stood within reach. Mom was busy cleaning, cooking, and washing during the day. In the evening, she sat on the couch to either read a book or watch TV. Dad loved the *Live with Regis and Kathie Lee* show, but no other shows were must-sees for him. Mom especially liked to watch old movies.

My parents' backyard was a gathering place for the ladies in the neighborhood to meet and chat. No one had a fence, so their grassy backyards merged into one big green place with my parents' yard in the center. Mom and Dad also had a patio.

Mom was sociable and always loved having friends over. She kept chairs on the patio for the neighbors, and often, one or more of them would stop by to chat on a warm summer evening. Even Dad occasionally joined the ladies, one of whom was married to Dad's partner in owning the *Falcon*.

Ivy was a close neighbor. Her backyard adjoined Mom's backyard. Ivy was a lovely person who always had a dog she doted on. Wilson was her last one. Ivy wouldn't allow Wilson to walk on the grass, so she carried him to her chair, and he sat on her lap.

Mom planted flowers under a big pine tree and placed colorful pinwheels among them to make a little park. The breezes blowing from the Atlantic Ocean into the yard made the pinwheels twirl almost constantly. (The house wasn't on the ocean, but it was close enough to catch the breezes.) When I visited, I joined the outdoor chats and was surprised every time by how much I enjoyed the company.

Mom took care of the yard. She pulled weeds:

> I just came in the house from weeding & I'm exhausted. I started Sun. afternoon. I did more last night & almost 3 hrs today. The weeds were taking over tho & your father wouldn't touch them. He said they were nice. I'm so afraid of the bugs tho, I have to take all my clothes & throw them in the hamper & take a bath as soon as I come in.

She tended their beautiful trees: two copper beech trees in the front and a mimosa tree on the side. I liked the mimosa tree so much that Mom gave me a starter from it one year. I planted it, and it took root and grew into a lovely mature mimosa tree in the yard of the house Kent and I owned in Ohio.

Every fall, Mom and Dad argued over raking leaves:

> I tried to get your father to rake the leaves around the yard. Your father said he won't do it until every last leaf is off all the trees, which will be never of course.

> It's a good day for raking leaves but I won't do it unless your father also goes out to do some. I don't mind helping but I'm not doing it alone. I told the neighbors too, so that if we're the only one with leaves, they know the reason.

Once in a while, Dad took on a project:

> Your father wants to build a compost box so he spent $60 on nails & lumber. I wanted to tell him

he could buy a lot of veggies for that money, but I knew he would come back with "I don't go on any trips." Then again, it's his money so he can spend it on foolish things.

Your father hurt his back. By the time he gets done with that compost heap, he could have bought a truckload of vegetables.

A year later, the happy outcome was the following:

We have a garden full of sunflowers that came up from the compost. Every day we have 2 little yellow birds come & eat the seeds. They're the same color as the sunflowers. I think they're finches.

Mom was an excellent cook, but Dad always found some problem with her meals (though, if you remember, the dog food he ate was "not bad"). Mom said,

I made ham for Easter. Your father wanted raisin sauce with it. I told him he should be tired of asking for it after 40 years. Geraldine said she made it once for him and he complained about it. He now weighs 230 pounds, the heaviest he's ever been. He really doesn't eat that much, he's just inactive. He sat all day reading or watching TV while I made the ham. He complained because he had to take out the cloves. I said sarcastically "Do you want me to do it?" He thought I really meant it and said that he'd do it himself.

Of course, Mom could be difficult too. At times, she nagged him mercilessly, and she had a temper.

When they were younger, Mom and Dad were always the first kids on the block to get new technology. In the early 1950s, we had a black-and-white TV with a small, round screen. My sister and I watched *The Howdy Doody Show* on it. We were thrilled when Mom took us to see Howdy Doody's touring show at a local theater. How many people can say they saw Flub-A-Dub in person? Dad's parents also had a TV, which my sister and I watched every Friday night when Mom went to the movies. At my grandparents' house, at 8:00 p.m., we watched *Mama*, a show about an early twentieth-century Norwegian American family living in San Francisco. At 9:00 p.m., we watched *The Big Story* about newspaper reporters. We went to bed when the Gillette boxing show came on at 10:00 p.m.

On Sundays, when we had dinner at my grandparents', we watched the singing cowboy Roy Rogers and sang "Happy Trails to You" along with him. In 1960, Mom and Dad had one of the first color TVs in the neighborhood. When they bought it, only baseball games and the Rose Bowl Parade were broadcast in color. Other shows were gradually added, until every show was broadcast in color. We watched the 1960 Winter Olympics on that modern TV. We had state-of-the-art television in that old house on Chestnut Street.

It took three trips to the appliance store to get the last TV Mom and Dad bought up and running. Since my parents didn't have cable at the time (it involved too many wires for Mom's taste), the TV had to be downgraded from the factory settings. Getting it to work frustrated Dad to no end. He finally got it running, and they learned to use the remote control, but that was as far as they went. Someone gave them a VCR, but neither of them ever used it. One time, after my nephew muted the sound on the TV, Mom watched it for a week with no sound rather than bothering anyone to get the sound back on. That was typical of Mom's generation. They lived with struggle and weren't demanding.

Dad was in his glory during the 1994 Olympics, which took

place in Lillehammer, Norway, and Mom wrote about the Olympic Games often:

> Your father and I watched the Lillehammer Olympics again last night and we enjoyed it. They have *so* many commercials tho.

> We watched the Olympics almost all weekend. Your father has it on day & night.

> Your father and I watched the Olympics again last night. Of course he spends most of his time criticizing the Americans for mispronouncing Norwegian names. Every time someone from Norway came on, he perked right up. Did you know that Lillehammer is smaller than Kingston in population?

> We watched the Olympics closing & of course it was beautiful.

Their mutual enjoyment of the Olympics was unusual. Typically, they argued or disagreed about almost everything, and they were highly competitive. They had fierce competitions over how many birthday cards each received and who would die first.

Mom always got more birthday cards because she herself sent a lot of cards. She would ask Dad how many he sent. The answer, of course, was zero. But that didn't stop Dad from complaining that she got more cards.

To stave off death, Mom walked two miles a day, and Dad took dozens of vitamins and supplements. He became interested in homeopathic remedies. By taking supplements, he thought he would live to be one hundred. (Mom always said Dad was gullible; he believed the hype.) Since Mom and Dad complained about each other so much, I don't know if their fifty-year marriage was filled with happiness as much as it was tolerance. They were loyal to each other and, for the most part, civil. Their relationship was just weird. Their fragile, contentious marriage ended when Dad unexpectedly died in his sleep. From then on, Mom lived alone, with regular visits from my sister and chats with the ladies in the backyard.

All through their marriage years, my sister and I watched my parents and learned to love equally two vastly different people. Then we ourselves married, had kids, divorced, married again, and met interesting people along the way.

As I mentioned, I met David, a Catholic priest, when I was taking classes in Bible history at the church. Shortly before Kent and I separated, I approached him for counseling about our marriage, which I knew was coming apart. After my divorce, David and I talked over coffee a few times and became friends.

To know what he looked like, imagine a traditional picture of Jesus: shoulder-length hair, short beard, and gentle eyes. Add intellect, kindness, and a soft voice, and you have him. We discovered we had a connection, a meeting of the minds. I had a need for coming to terms with divorce, and who better to provide it than someone who looked like the Lord and was a priest? After my divorce, my self-esteem was at its lowest. Then, to my surprise, David appeared to treasure me. He praised my choices and my childrearing skills. He boosted my ego every time we talked. He told me my kids were special and talented and had great potential—things every mother wants to hear—and he was sincere.

We listened to classical music. Occasionally, we went to a late movie. We talked about religion, relationships, agape love, and ethics. He introduced me to philosophers, such as Søren Kierkegaard, the mystical priest Pierre Teilhard de Chardin and his Cosmic Christ theories, and the martyred theologian Dietrich Bonhoeffer. To this day, I'm attracted to Bonhoeffer, a man of the cloth who plotted to assassinate Adolf Hitler. He reconciled the dichotomy by reasoning that Hitler's death would result in the most good. When jailed and deprived of his possessions, he grew and became more spiritual and more loving. He was a remarkable man. His book *Letters and Papers from Prison* reveals the person he was.

Since he was busy during the day, occasionally, David visited me at home in the evening. I also visited him at his residence. When I knew him, he worked at a retreat center, which was built like a small motel. It had a cafeteria and many guest rooms. The center was situated in a wooded area not far from my house. I often took the kids for walks on its lush green grounds.

One Saturday night, when David and I were at the retreat center, talking into the wee hours of the morning, I decided to sleep in one of the guest rooms. I went home early the next morning, in time for my weekly phone call with Mom at 9:30 a.m. (The kids were with Kent. Under terms of our divorce agreement, they spent every other weekend with him.) For some reason, Mom called earlier than usual on that particular Sunday. When she couldn't reach me, she was frantic with worry and almost called the police to look for me. I felt terrible for worrying her but shied away from telling her the truth about where I had been, because appearances might have given her the wrong impression. I told her I hadn't heard the phone. God forgive me!

My children got along well with David. He was good with children. After knowing him more than a year, I invited him to spend a few days with my parents in Massachusetts. I planned to visit them for a week and would drive there with the kids. David would fly out for a day or two.

I had talked about the plans to Mom. Before the trip, Mom wrote,

> I'm looking forward to your visit but I'm a little leery about David, but I guess you know what you're doing.

We stayed with my parents and had a nice visit. David and I took the kids on a two-hour ferry ride to Martha's Vineyard, an island off the coast famous for being Jackie Kennedy's home. We toured the island and fed seagulls while on the boat. I have a wonderful image in my mind of David holding Tracey up to reach the big white birds as they swooped in to take food out of her hands. It was a happy, family-like moment, but it couldn't last. David belonged to the church.

David introduced me to a religious community that was centered on Carmelite nuns and also included clergy and laypeople. The community was a new concept. It was reportable to the Vatican, and members were responsible for the upkeep of the nuns' convent and its grounds. In a ceremony at the diocesan cathedral, members were formally invested and pledged their commitment. I never joined, although I participated in its activities for a year or two. After my divorce, I needed company, adult conversation, and spirituality. Both David and the community provided those.

My daughter Lisa received her First Communion there. At the last minute, my parish church excluded Lisa from its First Communion class because I hadn't formally joined the church. (I did attend its weekly masses, and Lisa had taken pre-Communion training.) My mother's flight to Ohio was already booked. David saved the day. He arranged to say Mass at the community and gave Lisa her First Communion. It was an extra special day for her with the good Carmelite nuns, her mother, and her grandmother present.

The weekly community meeting consisted of scripture readings, meditation, and socializing. During the readings and meditations, anyone could freely say what he or she was thinking. The chapel was small, and the extemporaneous comments resonated. I never spoke up. Everyone was invited to write liturgical music, and I composed an alleluia that was often used.

The readings were followed by a social hour, and homemade food was served.

I was introduced to saints Teresa of Avila and John of the Cross, a mystic who wrote "The Dark Night of the Soul," a poem about reaching God after a time of spiritual emptiness. I related well to these mystics. During that time, I composed a reading that was used at my parish church at Thanksgiving Mass. The recognition was good for my soul. I felt that after the darkness of losing my marriage and self-esteem, I was coming into the light. After a long, dark night of the soul, I had hope.

I enjoyed the readings and the music, but I couldn't commit to a lifetime membership and doing things like helping with snow removal. I had my own snow to remove. In all honestly, I was there because of David and not a calling to a religious lifestyle. Unfortunately, the community was disbanded some years after I left. Members scattered, and the nuns returned to their cloisters. I was sorry to hear that. I thought the world was a better place with the community in it.

My friendship with David was restrictive; we kept it quiet for appearance's sake. In the 1970s, it was unheard of for a priest to have close friends, let alone a female friend. Although they knew we were friends, even my parents were uncomfortable with our relationship. But David was there for me at a time when I needed him. He offered kindness, spirituality, and hope. He taught me only good things and made me feel good about myself. It was another weird type of love, I guess. We haven't spoken in more than forty years, but I still remember his kindness—and Dietrich and the Cosmic Christ.

> We are not physical beings having a spiritual experience; we are spiritual beings having a physical experience.
> —Pierre Teilhard de Chardin

After my divorce from Kent, I was single for four years until I remarried. I didn't do much dating. Occasionally, I went to a party given by friends at work. One time, I was standing alone, and a stranger approached. "Couldn't get a date, huh? If I wasn't married, I'd date you," he said. His arrogance stunned me. Did I not have a say in whom I dated? I found him boring and uninteresting and wasn't at all attracted to him. But I did admire his confidence. I needed some of that!

I met my second husband, Scott, at work. He was athletic, with long legs and a torso that demanded shorter legs. If his legs had matched his torso, he would have been short like I was. As it was, he was almost six feet tall. His eyes were blue, and his hair was a dirty blond. He was handsome and younger than I by almost ten years.

I met him after work on a summer day, on the company's beautifully maintained grassy grounds, where softball was played on Friday afternoons. He was leaning on his car, drinking a beer, and asked me if I wanted to join his softball team. I had never played softball, but I was up for an adventure, so I said yes.

Scott was highly intelligent, which was what attracted me to him. After a ten-month courtship, we were married by a Presbyterian minister in a Jewish synagogue. No Catholic church would marry us since I had already married Kent in the church.

Scott and I thought we loved each other, but in retrospect, our marriage was more of a convenience than a love connection. I wanted someone to help raise the kids and take care of the house, and he wanted someone to make life easier for him. There wasn't much underlying affection. Nonetheless, we took marriage vows to love and honor each other.

I changed my last name to Scott's. Yet another identity for me. The kids, who still had Kent's last name, now had a last name different from mine, in spite of my previous efforts to keep our name the same. Eventually, the kids married, so in time, none of our names were the same.

I settled into marriage but soon found out that Scott had no interest in helping with the house. Also, he proposed keeping our finances separate and deemed that I would pay three-fourths of all expenses! He must have thought of me and the kids as his roommates. I talked him into merging our finances, and we agreed he would manage the books and pay the bills—an arrangement I would come to regret.

He didn't know anything about home maintenance and didn't want to learn. He watched sports on TV almost constantly; when he wasn't watching sports, he was playing softball, tennis, and golf. Having Scott was like having a third child. I used to tell him to consider donating his organs to someone who could use them; I would hook him up to the TV and an IV. Despite our differences, we made things work for more than twenty years.

We both believed that married people had an advantage on the job. There was a perception that they were more stable, able to commit, and likely to stay at the place. I poured myself into my career and did well. I worked long hours, while Scott casually oversaw things at home from the TV room. To Mom and my family, we looked like a happy couple, and I thought we were. He was good with the kids and developed good relationships with them. We were compatible and rarely argued. His parents enjoyed our company and visited often.

In time, I discovered that Scott kept secrets from both his parents and me. He waited months before telling his parents we were married, and after we married, he told me he had a chronic illness. He was sick as long as I knew him. I didn't realize how serious his illness was until he was diagnosed with stage-four cancer at the age of forty-three. He survived for a year and a half after the diagnosis but told his parents about the cancer only a month before he died. I didn't interfere with the relationship between Scott and his parents. I figured it was their business.

In the last month of Scott's life, his parents came to stay with us. I wouldn't deny him that comfort, although it gave us no privacy. Hospice set up a hospital bed for him in our living room.

On a crisp October day, his mother summoned a priest to our house to hear his confession. When I arrived home from work, he taunted me that he was going to heaven and I wasn't—a reference to our not being married in a Catholic church. Throughout his illness, I made a vow to myself not to upset him. I bit my tongue rather than responding to his taunt, but I was hurt that he would say that to me in one of our last conversations.

That night, his two closest friends and my daughters' families visited. It was a bit magical how everyone dear to him converged in our living room that night. His last evening on earth was a pleasant, happy one. He died a few hours after everyone left. He was forty-five years old. Although he had a few faults—don't we all?—I had made a commitment to him. I kept my vows, and I thought he had kept his.

Right after Scott died, I called the undertaker. Around two o'clock in the morning, I heard a knock at the front door. I expected that the undertaker had arrived. I opened the door to find a mysterious stranger who said he needed to get inside. He looked to be thirty to forty years old and had fresh blood on his head. He put his foot in the door to keep it open and tried to get in by pushing on it. The guy was stronger than I was, and I was worried he would break in. In the surreal situation, grieving and confused, I briefly imagined the stranger was Death, the Grim Reaper, coming for Scott's soul.

While the stranger and I were struggling in the doorway, the undertaker showed up and, mistaking the stranger for a relative, tried to open the door for him, but I cried repeatedly that I didn't know him. Finally, the undertaker—a big, burly bear of a man—heard me, walked the stranger back outside, and called the police. I never found out what the man wanted, but he got nothing from me. The undertaker got Scott's body.

As I grieved and sorted Scott's things, I discovered secrets he had kept from me. For one thing, he had spent all our money. I was broke. For another, it looked as if he had had a girlfriend. I spent days looking into things. I remembered unexplained phone calls and found suspicious photos, bank statements, and notes. It appeared he was supporting a young lady, including paying for her apartment and putting her through college. She was younger than my younger daughter.

I still grieved his loss, but I became angry and frightened. I had no idea what Scott had been up to. Had the girl been a diversion for him, or did he have a second family? There were no answers to any questions I had. He was gone. I didn't tell his parents because I didn't want to hurt them.

In planning his memorial service, his parents wanted more bells and whistles than I could afford. By then, I knew that Scott had left me broke. I had planned on a mass and some kind words. They wanted a choir, a pianist, and a luncheon for everyone who came. In the end, they paid for what they wanted, and Scott had a fine send-off. Heaven knows what they thought of me. But I felt better in knowing I had kept Scott's secrets and hadn't burdened his parents with them. I'm convinced I did the right thing. Since my kids had loved Scott and continued to miss him, I didn't burden them with my hurt either.

Gradually, I rebuilt my life. Scott's life insurance came through quickly. With Scott gone, I worked extra hard at my job and was promoted to department head. Within six months, I was financially secure, and within a year, I sold the house we had lived in and moved closer to my daughters. I bought a charming Arts and Crafts house in their city.

I asked myself, "How did I, an educated person, get myself into not one but two unhappy marriages?" I believe I used marriage to fill the emotional emptiness in my life. In looking back, I recalled that my father was emotionally distant. He never said he loved me or gave me an encouraging word. Since he took little interest in what I was doing, I had few expectations for finding love from him. I knew that Mom loved me. She knew what was going on in my life and supported me. But even she had some emotional impoverishment that didn't allow her to show affection.

Perhaps emotional detachment is why I felt like an alien when I was a little girl, waiting for my real parents to whisk me away to happiness. Perhaps I was waiting to feel loved. I had looked for love in two marriages and hadn't found it. I learned from my mistakes that I needed to fill my emptiness from within.

My sister, Geraldine, also had to deal with Mom's emotional issues. She had to break the news that she was expecting a baby with her second husband. We were all delighted, except for Mom.

> Geraldine informed us Sunday that she's pregnant. Needless to say I'm not too happy about it, but of course she didn't ask me. She said she and Richard are happy. He's already started to build baby things like a cradle.

Mom was never happy about new family members. I believe that if Mom had had her way, my sister and I would never have had children. Perhaps she had thought kids were out of the picture once she managed to raise Geraldine and me safely to adulthood. So whenever we announced we were expecting, she was miserable. "Oh no, not another one!" she would say. My sister and I knew Mom had anxiety. She would love the child once it had been born, but she would never stop worrying about it.

Communications between my mother and sister were cold while each came to terms with the news of my sister's coming baby and its effect on Mom. Mom wrote,

> I haven't seen or spoken to Geraldine since the day I found out about it. I guess I upset her, maybe she expected congratulations and I didn't give it.

> Geraldine said she hasn't called because she
> doesn't want to talk about her pregnancy. She
> said she has to think about her health. I told her
> I wouldn't pursue the subject.

My sister was strong and would have her baby with or without Mom's support, just as I had. But I was concerned about my mother. She was such a worrier.

Around that time, Geraldine's daughter, Leanne, announced that she too was pregnant. Mom was beside herself. There were so many things to worry about. She felt it was her personal responsibility to worry about everyone in the family.

Leanne considered all possibilities about how to handle the pregnancy. Social services provided support and counseling. After counseling, she ruled out abortion. Then she made her decision, a hard choice: adoption.

She had the option to choose the adoptive parents, based on their personalities, beliefs, ability to provide, upbringing, and more. She chose three couples whose profiles she liked and was leaning toward one couple in particular. A few weeks later, she learned that the potential father had lost his job. She felt sympathy but said she had to do what was best for the baby and chose another couple.

In her late months of pregnancy, Leanne left school to be tutored. She thrived under tutorship. She got excellent grades and graduated high school with high honors. She had a blue-eyed baby boy, whom she named Stephen Michael in her heart. Mom wrote,

> Leanne was going to feed the baby tonight. She had
> a hard time delivering him yesterday. I feel bad that
> she suffered. It sure was a high price to pay.

Leanne saw the baby for the last time at the adoption agency before they released him to his new family, who would give him a name and a home. She was distraught but not in despair. She believed she had made the right choice. Mom referred to the baby as Baby John Doe and prayed every day of her life that he was loved and cared for by his adoptive family.

When faced with a life-or-death situation, Leanne chose life. What courage it must have taken for this young girl to carry a baby to full-term, suffer the pains of childbirth, and then hand her baby over to a new family to be loved. She was conscientious and brave, one of the bravest young girls I have known, full of love and responsibility. Sometimes we find our heroes in unexpected places.

Leanne's baby went out into the word being loved by people he didn't know: his birth family, who were in his past, and his adoptive family, who were his future. Giving him up for adoption was a leap of faith. Baby John Doe was in God's hands, and God moves in mysterious ways.

In the end, despite our foibles, our family survived its struggles with love and its emotions and in the end had many happy outcomes. As my grandchildren grow older, they will have their own struggles, as every generation does. My advice to my grandchildren is not to rush into a relationship. Get to know the other person, and follow your head as well as your heart. The heart feels, but the head knows.

CHAPTER 8

Work Brings Salvation

*A*s a young adult, I more or less floated through life. I went to high school and then college. I got married and had children. With precious little thought, I went from one life experience to another based on society's expectations. I didn't consider who I was or what I needed to be true to myself and happy. I never planned on working full-time. I thought I would always be home with my children. But since I hadn't planned my life, fate made plans for me. After my first marriage ended in divorce, I was a single mother with two kids to support and a house to maintain. I was getting no alimony and only the minimal amount for child support. I had to find a full-time job to provide for myself and the kids. Landing a job meant I had to face reality. No more coasting. It turned out that in finding a job, I found my self-respect and my self-worth. Work was my salvation.

Seeking a job, on a friend's recommendation, I contacted an employment agency and discovered that a prestigious scientific company—one I had read about in college—was located just miles from where I lived. I applied for two different positions, was offered one of them, and accepted it. My chemistry degree opened a door for me that changed my life. Although I didn't appreciate it at the time, I'm thankful I chose a field that made me employable.

When I found a job, my older daughter was in school, and my toddler was still at home. My first order of business was to find a kind and reliable babysitter. I found a neighbor a few years younger than my mother who fit the bill. She had three children of her own and babysat others. The environment at her house was that of a big, happy family. There was lots of love in that house. In the morning, I scooped the kids up from their beds and drove them to the sitter in their pajamas. My babysitter was kind enough to feed the kids breakfast and get them dressed. The fact that I'd found a good babysitter was a big relief to me, but it didn't assuage my guilt for leaving my kids. Good mothers were expected to be full-time moms, not full-time workers.

On my first day of work, I was nervous and felt I was being swallowed up by a corporate world I knew nothing about. I was jumping into a rabbit's hole. I sensed I was losing some of my freedom, but I wondered if I would also lose my humanity as I entered the nine-to-five world. My mind was used to being filled with church teachings and philosophers. My days had been filled with kids and playdates. How would work change me?

The company's campus consisted of two modern, boxlike buildings, one of which had exterior latticework painted metallic gold, which gave it an appearance of richness. Inside the buildings, eight-foot square offices lined the hallways like monks' cells in an abbey. It was nicely appointed, with plants and paintings popping up here and there.

I found out that more than twelve hundred people worked there, and I soon discovered that the majority had been A students, as I had. I wasn't special; I was one among many, a stranger in a strange land.

For the first three years, I drove the twelve miles to work in tears. I hated leaving my kids. Often, I composed bad poetry in my head as I battled the traffic, dealt with my guilt, and faced the pressures of my new life. Upon seeing the body of a dog, I composed the following:

Today on the northbound freeway I met
The battered, torn carcass of somebody's pet,
Its food in the dish at home going stale.
I guessed that this morning it last wagged its tail.

However, I soon discovered that work suited me. It gave me financial security and opportunities to be creative and make social connections. While my chemistry was a bit rusty, it enabled me to quickly learn the job. It turned out I really did have an aptitude for chemistry.

The company that employed me created online databases for scientists to find information about new research. When I started working (almost fifty years ago), research findings were typically published in the hard-copy literature of the day, primarily in journals. You can think of a journal as a magazine with chapters written by experts in the field. My initial task was to review the journals to find research papers suitable for inclusion in the scientific databases.

There were about twenty-five people in my group, and most of us were about the same age. We each had a small office area, and our work spaces were separated by brightly colored moveable panels (red, yellow, and royal blue). It was an early use of the open-office concept, and it worked well. The openness allowed easy communication about the job, and I started forming friendships with my peers. I also developed appropriate relationships with management. I had never been managed before, but I had had teachers, and I had been married, so relating to the managers wasn't difficult. They were knowledgeable and friendly. The atmosphere was highly professional. After a short time, my job performance was top-notch, and the job paid well. If I wasn't with my kids every day, at least I was getting paid well for being away from them. I stayed for five years in that area. Mom's letters continued to arrive weekly and always cheered me up. She reminded me of my opportunities:

> When I was growing up, I didn't have the choices women do today. I don't remember a woman doctor or dentist. Women have made great progress in the working world.

Thanks to Mom, I never felt I couldn't do a job because I was a woman, and thanks to my new job, I was feeling more confident in my abilities. My confidence continued to grow as I moved into a project management position within the company. As a project manager, I supported the people, workflow, and computer systems associated with database building.

The new position involved learning a whole new set of skills and working with a different set of people. In retrospect, it was the position that gave me the most opportunities for exploring my creativity. It entailed problem-solving and finding solutions. I recall learning how to chart workflows using industry-standard symbols that represented documents, storage devices, computer programs, decision points, and so on. I interviewed people to find out what they needed to do their jobs and then charted the necessary workflows. I helped to design computerized systems that made the workflow more efficient. Programmers and engineers then built the systems. Often, after a new computer system was built, I wrote user manuals and designed training courses to teach people how to use it. I was a good teacher and received several company awards for my accomplishments in that area. I also wrote several technical papers that were published in well-known journals. This was before the internet, but I believe if you search certain databases hard enough, you can find those papers listed under my two married names.

I handled some big projects well, earned promotions, and

made a name for myself. I learned how to handle stress—in fact, I thrived on it. I became a workaholic, and I became ambitious. I knew I could handle a project well, so I sought more challenging work and higher positions. As I worked my way up the corporate ladder, desktop technology was introduced. This gave me an opportunity to head up a project that was to last for ten years. The project completely replaced the computer systems used to create the databases and affected hundreds of people. As usual, I worked with the people who designed the systems and the people who used them. Then I helped to create workflows and developed and conducted training sessions. The project was a success, and so was I.

After working for more than twenty years in technical positions, I was promoted into a management position in an area I knew well: computer system oversight. The job involved keeping the database-building systems working and running on time. We had a high success rate and avoided system breakdowns that could have had disastrous consequences. But our work was done behind the scenes. In general, we weren't praised for averting disasters that didn't happen, because those successes were invisible. It's hard to win awards for disasters prevented. In that position, I learned not to expect praise for everything I did. Doing a job well was a reward unto itself.

The work was highly technical and complicated, but I thought that management of it was a piece of cake. My staff were highly skilled professionals who knew what needed to be done and did it. Sometimes a manager has to step back and let people do their jobs. In managing that group, the hardest thing I had to do was divvy up the salary dollars among those high achievers.

After a few years, I moved into a more challenging management position in which I worked closely with people and faced their issues head-on. I had both good and problematic employees, several of whom I had to counsel and ultimately let go. I found it difficult to fire people. I knew I would be disrupting their lives in a major way, and I didn't know how they would handle the news. Problem employees were given every opportunity to turn things around. Letting them go was a last resort, and fortunately, it didn't happen often. Most of my staff tried to do good work, but I often had to intercede to keep them on track.

Finally, I was promoted to a department head. As a department head, I reported to a division head, who reported to the president of the company. I was pretty high up on the corporate ladder and proud of my success. My boss and I were companionable. We worked well together and collaborated on many successes. I had sixty to seventy people reporting to me and managed a multi-million-dollar budget. In that position, I was always on the lookout for a better way to do things, and I helped to implement many changes that saved the company money. In time, my department ran like a well-oiled machine.

The people at my place of work were from many countries across the globe so the world's scientific research could be found and read. There were people from Germany, Russia, China, Japan, and other countries in the Americas, Europe, and Asia. Locally, we were known as a little United Nations. While there were typical workplace issues, for a large multinational group to work well together was a credit to the management.

The grounds of the company had acres of well-tended green grass, walkways, and trees. A river flowed along the eastern edge of the property, where picnic tables were set up. Before I retired, a grand pavilion was built on the grounds for meetings, receptions, and the like. I had my retirement party in the pavilion.

My fifth-floor corner office offered good views. To the east was the river, which froze over in the winter and on which scullers rowed their boats in the summer. To the south were the skyscrapers of downtown.

Every day my lunch buddies and I would eat in the cafeteria, take a walk through the trees, and return by the river. Being outside in the fresh air was good revival for the afternoon's desk work. On Saturdays during the summer months, the company hosted concerts on its grounds. They were conducted by the local symphony and included classical and popular music. I enjoyed the concerts under the stars. I'd always appreciated Gershwin, Porter, Kern, and other composers. A band shell was set up, and hundreds of tables were set before it. Along with general seating on the lawn, there was room for fifteen thousand attendees. The events were well liked and well attended every year.

As a department head, I hosted a few front-row tables. To me, hosting was pudding on the cake of accomplishment since only key management got to do it. I had popped out of the rabbit's hole and was Alice in Wonderland. At the tables, delicious food was catered, and all the wine you could drink was available. I appreciated that and drank my fill. I'm glad I wasn't on the wagon then.

I especially remember one table I hosted. Among other guests, I had invited a husband and wife who both worked for me. They were delightful company, and we had a lovely evening listening to the music in perfect summer weather. They spoke proudly of their youngest son, who had recently married and moved to Colorado. Their son and his wife had planned to take a flight excursion that morning to see the mountains, and my employees were a little concerned that they hadn't heard from them. The other guests and I tried to allay their fears. We suggested many reasons why their son hadn't yet called them.

Back at work on Monday, we found out what had happened: a plane crash. Their son and his wife had both died when their small plane crashed. At the time of the concert, when we were enjoying ourselves and trying to keep hope alive, the young people were already dead, and their poor bodies were strewn on a mountain side. It was a sad and sobering experience. My joy at hosting a table paled in comparison to their grief over losing a son. I attended the memorial service, and I remember the boy's mother saying, "I lost my baby boy." How fragile life is, with babies lost and babies born, darkness and light, despair and redemption. I witnessed all of them and continued to learn.

By the end of my career, I was working eight hours a day at the facility and four hours a night from home thanks to computer networking, a technology that had become available. I worked every day and every weekend. Even when I took a day of vacation, I worked from home as much as possible. Eventually, I started getting sick on a somewhat regular basis, and I was often absent, although even then, I worked from home. I never took a sick day unless I was too ill to go into the office. I never gave less than 100 percent. My doctor attributed my frequent illnesses to stress. I was working too hard and was approaching burnout. Mom wrote,

I hope your job isn't giving you too much stress.

Sure hope you're feeling better today.

The stress and related illnesses planted a seed. I started thinking about retirement. No job, no matter how fulfilling, was worth getting sick over.

I had a special relationship with my secretary. During those stressful times, she gave me much-needed support and helped to keep my spirits up. Notably, she organized a surprise party for my sixtieth birthday. At least fifty people attended, including Mom and my sister. We took photos, which are precious to me today, especially one with my Mom, my sister, my two daughters, and me.

To top off the celebration, my kind secretary had taken up a collection and bought me a Himalayan cat. What a risk she had taken, but I loved cats and had room for a kitten. She drove me to the breeder, and I picked out my kitten. I named him Richard Parker after the Bengal tiger in *Life of Pi*. (The tiger got his name from a clerical error—he was incorrectly named as the hunter who found him drinking at a pool; the hunter was named Thirsty.)

Rich proved to be a lovely cat and lived with me well past my retirement to the age of fourteen. He loved to sleep in the sunlight, and I look for him when the sun shines on his favorite spot on the floor.

During my long career, I dated two people at work, including Scott, who I married. I liked the first man, but he rejected me because I had kids. He seemed interested in me but consulted his brother, a priest, about the kids. The priest advised him to move on, possibly because I couldn't be married in a Catholic church. Scott didn't mind the kids; in fact, he liked them—a redeeming quality.

When Scott died, I was given a week off work to grieve. It was a time of bereavement and reflection. I had experienced many ups and downs. I had gone from a bright and energetic college student to an unhappy housewife who didn't like herself. I experienced the death of a husband, but I found high-flying success at work and improved self-esteem. But something was lacking. I had yet to find happiness from within. Something had always defined me: school, marriage, or work. Who was I at heart?

Life of Pi shows that our challenges are what help to define us.[3]

> What greater challenge can there be than trapped with a ferocious tiger? More so, if that tiger is one's own fear, anxiety, depression, desolation, and despair. It is our faith that helps us cross the cruel and endless sea.

At the age of sixty-two, I decided to take early retirement. That was the earliest age at which I could collect Social Security benefits. I was tired and stressed out and believed I had given the company my best efforts. I had started work when I was young and scared. During my long career, I had acquired maturity and strength. Now it was time to leave.

---

[3] *Psychology Today*, Nov. 26, 2012.

I wondered what I would find in the next phase of my life without work to keep me occupied. For more than thirty years, my work had defined me. My sense of value related to how well I did on the job. I'd had a distinguished and fulfilling career, and I retired with a generous pension. Mom's attention to my early grades and my diligent work in college had paid off.

I summoned my strength and crossed the sea to the next shore: retirement. The first thing I noticed about retirement was that it blurred my sense of time. I didn't know what day it was without clues. Going from a day of structure and routine to one that had no boundaries jarred the senses. I always liked order and predictability. In those early days of retirement, I was adrift like Pi on his raft.

I helped with the grandkids as much as I could, picking them up from school, bringing them forgotten lunches or lunch money, and volunteering in their classrooms. My active grandson, Derek, required more attention than a teacher could give him, so I went to class with him almost every day for his early grades. While helping Derek, I was surprised how easily I connected with the kids and how I was able to teach them things.

One day, when I wasn't at school, out of curiosity, my grandson put his finger into an electric pencil sharpener. He wasn't seriously injured, but word spread about what he had done. My heart ached for that poor boy, who was doing the best he could with what he had been given. Eventually, my daughter got him a spot in an academy known for schooling kids on the spectrum, and he did well there. He was taught according to his abilities, not a curriculum.

When my grandson transferred to the academy, my volunteering came to an end. I talked to Mom on the phone every day and visited her several times a year. By then, I was older, and driving had become as onerous to me as flying. Since flying took less time, when I did travel, I flew, but I did so with intense fear. I might have visited more often had I not been so afraid to fly. Fear kept me grounded.

Mom had an intense fear of spiders. If she saw a spider, she was in a state of panic until the spider was removed. I explained my fear of flying to her like this: "Imagine you're sitting on a plane and have a spider on your lap for the entire flight." Mom well understood what my fear was like, and she never pressured me to visit. But I wish I had overcome my fear and visited her more often.

Thus, my early days of retirement were filled with family. I was happy enough with my life, but two short years later, Mom died, throwing my life into a tailspin and testing my mettle.

As I mentioned, Mom got a job at Cherry's when my sister and I were in our teens. She applied for work over the Christmas holidays and was asked to stay on when an older employee took sick. She stayed for more than thirty years.

I got my work ethic from my mother. Reading her letters, I saw her pride in her work and her loyalty to her coworkers. She had a clear sense of self and never cut corners. To her, that would have been cheating. When she was on the job, she gave 100 percent. Mom worked for thirty years in a job that had some similarities to my own: the need for employees to be productive and the related stress. Mom didn't make money like I did, but she worked hard, handled the stress well, and made a wealth of long-lasting friends.

Shopping at the Cherry and Webb department store was like stepping back in time. Both staff and customers were well groomed, civilized, and polite. Once, it was the largest fashion store in the city, with five floors of merchandise. It was well appointed, clean, and classy. Today the store Cherry and Webb exists only in memory. Through Mom's letters, I followed its slow demise.

> It's raise time in Cherry's. I haven't been called in
> yet but all the girls are disappointed. The raises
> are very small & some didn't even get one. You're
> supposed to get new charge accounts for the store
> & if you don't get enough, no raise.

I think of Cherry's like Grace Brothers in the PBS television show *Are You Being Served?* It had a grace and elegance that can't be found in modern shopping experiences. Customers had personal customer service. The staff knew their customers. Shopping was social and special, and there were no long checkout lines. Over the years, Mom worked in the children's department and in ladies' lingerie. As teenagers, my sister and I knew she was getting ready for work when we smelled her perfume drifting from her makeup counter in the master bathroom. It was the last step in her ritual. She did her hair, then her makeup, and finally her perfume. In contrast, I once went to work in a T-shirt and jeans I had slept in. Mom talked about her job in many letters.

> When we did inventory, we had a big stock shortage. They want us to watch the customers, yet last week Mary was on vacation & they didn't have anyone cover for her in the jewelry department. You know how easy it is to steal jewelry. It's small & it isn't tagged & yet they left the dept. empty. The girl on cosmetics is supposed to watch it but they get commission on selling cosmetics, so they couldn't care less about the jewelry. Of course we've been through this before, the bosses are all gung ho to fix things & then they lose interest. I have to go to a meeting on Friday about employee theft, there goes my hair appointment.

I love America and am glad I was born in this country, where anything is possible. America thrives on energy and hard work. Mom believed anything was possible, and she worked hard with boundless energy. She personified the land of our births.

America started to change in the 1960s. The Vietnam War was unpopular, and there were protests against it. We started to lose our unquestioning faith in government and, along with it, our innocence as a people. We were like children growing up and questioning our parents. Technology took relentless leaps. We treasured material things, and we couldn't buy them fast enough. Shopping needed to be quick. The tearooms of high-end department stores were closed down. Patrons didn't have time for tea. Shopping went on the to-do list and stopped being a leisurely experience.

Mom's store gradually lost business to the suburban malls, which offered amenities the downtown stores didn't have. At the malls, you were protected from the weather, and you could get from store to store quickly. The downtown stores were becoming relics of the past, just as the malls of today are competing with online suppliers. Cherry's situation wasn't unusual. The building and the staff were gradually downsized until only the main floor was open for business. Mom wrote,

> The store was open last Sunday & didn't make enough to pay for the electricity.

> Downtown business is terrible. Yesterday all the girls in Cherry's had their hours cut. That won't be any hardship on me, because I don't want to work too many hours. But I feel sorry for the girls who really need it.

The job turned out to be significant in Mom's life. It gave her a social outlet and a reason to dress up, do her hair, and wear makeup. It paid next to nothing but gave her a few dollars of her own. Mom left the job when she was seventy years old. She continued to see the girls from Cherry's until her final illness. They went to lunches, showers, parties, and other social events and often talked on the phone. Mom wrote,

> One of the women that worked in Cherry's died and my hairdresser Jane knew her. She picked up

Anita & I & we went to the wake. We had a great time. I almost felt guilty because all the girls from Cherry's were there & we had a social hour.

I'm going to have 5 or 6 of the girls from Cherry's for lunch. I'm planning on making those open faced sandwiches that Nanny used to make. I thought I could make egg salad & tuna salad & cream cheese & olive & sea food salad. I thought I'd have ham, roast beef & cheese also. I'll make some coleslaw. Some chips & dessert should finish it off.

In America and elsewhere, people are judged on their looks, and everyone wants to be good looking. One of the girls who worked at Cherry's had a single tooth in her mouth, and it was as plain as day. She was well liked and known as One Tooth behind her back. One day she came into work, and the tooth was gone. The girls were in a tizzy. But her nickname lived on. Whenever Mom mentioned her in one of her letters, she added "the girl that I work with, she has one tooth" after her name.

Sun. afternoon we went to Ellen's house (girl that I work with, she has one tooth). Her son-in-law breeds parakeets and he had a baby ready for Carl. They were white, blue & grey. He wouldn't take any money for it but I gave his little boy $10. The man has been out of work since March.

Ellen survived in a world that treasured beauty. She never talked about her tooth, and others learned not to ask her about it. It was part of her life and proved that the world had room for more than just pretty people. One Tooth was a happily married woman. When her husband died, she mourned him for years.

I called Ellen & asked her if she wanted to go out. She doesn't go to too many places since her husband died. She likes to go to the craft stores & she has to depend on someone to take her. This will be my good deed for the day because I'm not that crazy about driving.

Ellen and her one tooth had found true love, unlike me, who had found two unhappy marriages with all my teeth intact. I bet Ellen didn't feel like an alien from another planet either. She accepted who she was, whereas I was always trying to be better, prettier, and more loved.

Mom loved people and valued friendship. She was an energetic little person. She had the energy needed to keep many friends. She phoned them, sent birthday cards, invited them to lunch, and went on outings with them. I'm more aloof, like my father. Give me a book to read, and I'm happy. Mom often wrote about her friends in her letters:

> I helped a girl that I work with move into the Tripp Towers (senior living). She has a son who must be very selfish. He went on vacation & never offered to help her move. She has a small family but no one came to help her. I was tired & I really didn't feel like helping her, but now I'm glad I did. She was *so* nervous about the front door & the elevators, but with me along she said she felt better.

> I should have a busy day. Adele & I are taking Ellen to lunch for her birthday. Before we eat we're going to Buttonwood Park to get tickets for their Christmas party. Then after we eat, we're going shopping. Then I baked a cake for Ellen,

so I thought we would come back here for cake
& coffee.

Adele was one of Mom's closest friends. They met at Cherry's, where Adele worked at the candy counter, and became lifelong friends. They did things together that friends did back then before social media changed how we relate to one another. They went shopping, had lunch, and made birthday cakes for each other. They phoned each other often, not only to keep in touch but also to make sure the other was okay. They did favors for one another, shared food, took turns driving to the doctor, and so on. Despite their different backgrounds, they had a give-and-take friendship.

Adele was born in Belgium and had a difficult childhood because of the German occupation during World War II. Throughout her life, she had a pessimistic outlook and sorrowful memories of war-torn Belgium. Mom was the yin to her yang since Mom always tried to present a happy face to her friends. She believed that no one wanted to hear about your troubles or aches and pains. Mom tried to be bright and cheery in company.

> Adele & Carl both came yesterday. After we ate
> we went to see *Saving Private Ryan*. I didn't think
> Adele would want to go because she doesn't like
> to talk about the war, her country was under
> German occupation. Now I'm a big Tom Hanks
> fan. That movie made you wonder about war &
> all those lives lost. We should have only women in
> power. I don't think they would want their sons to
> go to war. I remember when the Sullivan brothers
> were all killed on the same ship.

Adele was a tiny person with short, curly hair who always walked like she was in a hurry to get somewhere. She had a pronounced European accent. She was a big baker, but she was also a big smoker, so her cakes sometimes tasted like cigarettes. Whenever Adele visited, she brought baked goods. Mom quietly sampled her food before serving it to make sure it didn't taste like smoke.

Since Adele lived alone, Mom took extra care to keep her close; Mom made sure she had company over the holidays. Their friendship was forever, and it had all started at work.

> I feel sorry for Adele. She has one daughter and they don't see each other. I told her she should come here for Christmas & she started to cry & she's not one to cry easily. I can't see her being alone on Christmas.

Despite her smoking, Adele was a healthy person until her final illness, which, unfortunately, lasted several years. We never knew what was wrong with her. She didn't want to talk about it.

> Adele called & said she had to go to the doctor's & she couldn't drive. The doctor is setting up an appointment for an MRI, he thinks there's something wrong around her liver. We were at the doctor's office for about 2 hours. On the way home she asked if I would stop to get her some ginger ale. That's about the only thing that agrees with her.

Adele had been having stomach pains for more than a year. She had tests, was hospitalized, and recovered. Then the cycle started again. Throughout her illness, Mom often helped her, although Adele told a mutual friend that she was getting no help from anyone. Mom overlooked whatever hurt she might have felt, because she knew Adele wasn't herself. In her later years, Mom was full of grace and forgiveness. Her life struggles had taken the edge off her anxiety about life.

Adele's health continued to deteriorate to the point where she could hardly walk. She was stubborn and wouldn't call her doctor. On one occasion, when Mom couldn't reach her on the phone, Mom called the police to check on her. Adele was fit to be tied and complained that the police broke her door to get in.

In the end, Adele died alone. Her death was discovered after a neighbor reported a bad smell coming from the house. The obituary said she'd died on July 3, the day her body was found, but Mom thought she'd died on June 29, the day she last talked to her.

When you think of it, everyone dies alone. You must make the journey by yourself. It is inevitable. Adele left her mark on our family. Mom wrote this story about my nephew Matthew:

> Matthew left his dishwashing job because he's working full-time on another job. He didn't know how to leave so he told them there was a family tragedy. They called Geraldine to see what was wrong & of course she didn't know what they were talking about. When Matthew got home she asked him what the family tragedy was & he said, "Adele."

I can imagine the loneliness Mom felt after Adele died. She was the last of the old girls from Cherry's. By then, Dad was gone, as was Tillie, Mom's beloved sister. Like me, Mom had her children and grandchildren. But her old friends were dying, and work was a distant memory.

Throughout her life, Mom tended friendships like gardens. She kept in touch and nurtured them. My father couldn't understand why she was so well liked.

> I had a phone call from a friend who has an eye problem. She wanted a shoulder to cry on. I

listened & when she said good-bye, she said, "I love you Dot." I said I love you too. Your father wanted to know what that was all about. I told him. He said, "You have quite a few women telling you they love you & I can't understand why, you're not that great!"

I made a plate of leftover ham & brought it over to my neighbor Raymond. I feel so sorry for him, I talk to him a lot when I take my walks. He's so alone & he told me the other day he has one sister and she's called him twice since his wife died over 10 years ago. Your father couldn't understand why I was bringing him the ham. It didn't cost me anything & I hope I put a little joy in his life.

Mom's job was an adventure. My job was a career. In both our cases, work was our salvation. It gave Mom a reason to get out of the house and to get dressed up in the frills that she had loved from an early age. At work, Mom was the star she had always wanted to be, well liked, well dressed, and as pretty as a peacock. She made a wealth of friends, and she held them closely. When Mom retired, she kept her friends. Work gave me a sense of worthiness and competency: it reminded me that I had value and was worthy of respect. I rediscovered my capabilities: I was a leader and a problem solver. In the end, my work gave me a pension to live on during retirement. But when I left work, my friends stayed behind. They went with the job. There were a few efforts to keep in touch, but the friendships fizzled out when the situation changed. At home in my Arts and Crafts bungalow, I missed my friends.

CHAPTER 9

You're an Addict

Forty million Americans ages twelve and older—more than one in seven people—abuse or are addicted to nicotine, alcohol, or other drugs. This is more than the number of Americans with heart conditions, diabetes, or cancer.[4]

I've personally struggled with addiction. I've seen others struggle. Addictions likely caused the deaths of several close family members, namely my father and my aunt Tillie, who smoked heavily, so it's an important subject to me. I want to emphasize that I'm not an expert. Everything in this chapter is anecdotal, based on my experience and observation.

My father and his father both drank to excess when they came home from fishing trips. I don't remember Dad's father drinking, but Mom told me that he was an alcoholic and that one drink would set him off. Mom's father, Pop, liked to have a few beers too. They loosened him up. Even Mom had a small drink of whiskey every night to help her sleep. From a young age, I was used to

---

[4] Partnership to End Addiction, *Fast Facts About Addiction*, https://drugfree. org/article/fast-facts-about-addiction/, accessed Aug. 22, 2020.

seeing people drinking. I had an addictive personality. I drank for more than thirty years.

Possibly I inherited the alcohol gene from my father. During his younger days, Dad and the fishing crews headed to the bars as soon as they cashed their paychecks. They celebrated their safe return and anything else that came to mind. They got uproariously drunk. Obviously, Mom wasn't happy about that behavior, and she took Dad to task over his drinking many times. Although getting drunk was Dad's decision, Mom felt shamed. She tried to get him to stop.

One time, Mom criticized Dad's drinking while he was still under the influence, and he started slapping her. He backed her into a corner up against a kitchen towel rack, where she cowered. She was almost a foot shorter than he was and weighed about a hundred pounds less than he did. It was an unfair fight. My sister and I cried and tried to pull him off her. When his anger was spent, he calmly went off to sleep. Mom took my sister and me to his mother's house until things calmed down. Mom asked us if she should leave him, and we both cried, "No, Mom, please don't!"

I later wondered if we consigned her to years of unhappiness with our father. I don't think we did. Back then, Catholics didn't divorce, and that was the only time Mom ever brought up the subject. He never hit her again, no matter how drunk he got. He wasn't a violent man, but alcohol changed him. For some reason, he was a mean drunk.

When he was drinking, my father got mugged and knocked unconscious, had his pay stolen, and slept it off in jail a few times. I worried about him both when he was out at sea and when he came home. In my mind, my father was truly home when the binge was over, not when the boat pulled into port.

Our family never forgot the time he fell off one of the piers, nearly drowning and breaking a leg. After a night of drinking, he was trying to find his boat to spend the night in. He slipped and fell about ten feet into the greasy water around the pilings.

If it hadn't been for two policemen who were following him, he would have drowned. They saw him fall off the pier and quickly hoisted him out. Mom tried to keep the news off the radio but was unsuccessful. "Maybe they won't know he was drunk," I naively said.

Mom replied, "Who else but a drunk would be staggering around the piers at three o'clock in the morning?"

She sent the rescuers a fruit basket, and a few friends mentioned they were glad he was safe, and that was the end of it—except Dad had to use crutches for a while. Since he was a big man, using crutches was uncomfortable for him, but Mom had no sympathy.

I started drinking heavily when Scott died, although I drank when he was alive too. Mom was the first to point out that I might have a drinking problem. I was in my fifties. I didn't think I had a problem, but I couldn't stop at one drink. I had to have up to three or four. Mom never approved of the way I drank, and whenever I drank in front of her, I felt her eyes on me. It was inevitable that she would say something. She thought I drank too much too quickly, and I probably did.

I started drinking lightly when I was married to Kent. A girlfriend and I got in the habit of having a few glasses of wine after taking our kids on playdates. That was when I discovered alcohol's therapeutic properties. A glass or two of wine put me in a better mood and enabled me to better cope with a marriage that was going bad, at least for a little while.

After my divorce, I was still drinking a couple of glasses of wine a day—still not too bad. Then, after I married Scott, I added beer and whiskey to the list, so I had a full repertoire.

Drinking relieved my anxieties. I was always afraid of something. If the kids were five minutes late in coming home, I was in a panic. Looking back, I realize my separation anxiety was rearing its head, but at the time, I wasn't analyzing my motives. Drinking made it easier to deal with my frequent panic and anxiety attacks. I drank to take the edge off, not because I liked the taste. It helped that alcohol was easy to obtain and was legal.

I also drank when I was under stress, which was almost all the time. I was raising teenagers and had a full-time job and a young husband who didn't help around the house. Moreover, Scott's parents visited often. Prior to their visits, I cleaned the house from top to bottom to get everything ready for them. I was responsible for their visits, not Scott. Sometimes I got tired and went off to hide in the bedroom with a big glass of whiskey. In addition, I continued drinking as my stress at work increased along with my responsibilities. By the time my job was taking off, I was drinking regularly and heavily.

I thought things were under control. I never drank in the morning or during work; drinking never affected my job. I drank in the evening; I had my first glass of wine as soon as I walked in the door and my last when I went to bed. I also drank on weekends. But I was hurting no one.

I was aware of my drinking and somewhat concerned about it. A little voice kept telling me I was drinking too much. I knew why I drank, but I wondered if my reasons for drinking were actually excuses. Was I an addict? I looked up the definition of *alcoholic* many times, trying to find reasons why I wasn't one. I should have realized that it didn't matter what the definition was. If I was or wasn't an alcoholic, if I had a reason for drinking or didn't, I was a problem drinker. I refused to face the problem head-on. My needs for anxiety relief were too great.

When Scott got sick and was hospitalized, Mom visited me and saw I was drinking. One day we planned on visiting Scott at the hospital and then meeting his parents for dinner. Mom refused to go because I had had a few drinks and would be driving. Although I attempted to cajole her, she was firm about her decision. I had to explain her absence at the dinner table. I thought she was being overly cautious. My husband had cancer; if I couldn't drink then, when could I drink?

Usually, I was careful not to drive after I had been drinking—well, after excessive drinking. I thought nothing of driving after just a few drinks. On one occasion, after a night out with some softball teammates at a place where there was lots of booze but nothing to eat, I drove home, even though I was so drunk I couldn't focus my eyes. My guardian angel worked extra hard that night. I hate drunk drivers as much as anyone, but I have been a drunk driver. It was grace that protected me and others who were in my path.

After Scott died, I moved to my Arts and Crafts house. When I opened the pantry door, I discovered a supply of spirits left by the previous owner. All the bottles had been opened and used to some extent. The bottles were so old they were covered in dust. Without giving it a second thought, I finished every bottle. I look back on that and wonder why I wasn't concerned about contamination. I probably convinced myself that the alcohol would have killed any germs left in the bottles. I know how I used to think. But looking back on it, I think that was a pretty sad thing to do. I could have been drinking rat poison for all I knew.

Once, I fell down the stairs in my house from the second floor to the first. I stepped out of my bedroom door in the middle of the night to use the restroom. In the doorway, I got dizzy, and instead of falling left into the bathroom, I fell right into the air and down the steps. I had been drinking. What a horrible feeling I had when I floated into the air, knowing I would inevitably hit the stairs, and there was nothing I could do about it. Luckily, I have good bones—and a good guardian angel—and only bruised myself. To explain the bruises on my arms and legs, I told people I had tripped over a cat in the dark. Good grief, I blamed the poor cat.

During my trips to Massachusetts to visit Mom, when I drank her alcohol, she kept track of how many drinks I had. She remembered how many drinks I had when even I didn't know. That annoyed me to no end. I used to wonder if she would ever lose her excellent memory. Weren't old people supposed to forget things? I never wished Mom to have memory problems, but they would have been a way out of my dilemma. It was nonsensical thinking to wish away a problem. Still, it shames me to think of it.

One day I became disheartened. I always loved visiting my little grandson Derek. On one visit, when I came in the door, he ran over to the refrigerator in his little footed onesie to get me a beer. "Want a beer, Nana?" he asked. *This is pathetic*, I thought. A toddler knew my drinking habits. From then on, whenever I came to visit, he got me a beer.

Another time, Derek spent the night with me so we could get up early to watch a parade. I was extra nervous when the grandkids spent the night, had more to drink than usual, and woke up with a hangover. Derek had already gotten up and fixed his breakfast and was watching TV. Once again, I thought I was pathetic. I was a grandmother in my fifties getting drunk with a small child in my care. However, since Derek and I saw the parade and survived his overnight stay with no ill effects, I didn't stop drinking. The pull was too strong, and no one had gotten hurt.

Finally, something happened at work that made me take notice. I had a few drinks at a work-related dinner and a brief, friendly conversation with my boss. The next day, he asked if I had a drinking problem. I was indignant and also a little scared. I didn't think I'd had too much to drink at the dinner, so why was he asking that question? I must have been missing something.

I drank for two more years—through Mom's illness and death. But then a miracle happened: two months after Mom died, I stopped drinking cold turkey. I hadn't been planning on stopping. In fact, I had all the excuses I needed to drink more than ever: I had retired from my job, I lived alone, and I had lost my husband and my mother. But I knew I was skating on thin ice. All the ingredients were there for my problem drinking to turn into raging alcoholism. I didn't want that to happen. I had children and grandchildren who needed me.

Something made me ask the question "What good can come

from drinking?" I couldn't come up with anything good, although I came up with a lot of bad things that could happen. At that moment, it was as if the sun burst through the clouds. I could see clearly. I had no yearning to drink. I listened to the small voice in my head that I had been ignoring, recognized that I had a drinking problem, and quit my habit on the spot.

The change was abrupt, and I had no rational explanation. It was supposed to be hard to break an addiction. I didn't find it hard at all. I'm convinced that some higher power interceded on my behalf.

I wished Mom knew that I had stopped drinking. It would have made her so happy. But deep down, I think she might have helped me. She had been in heaven for two months, enough time to make friends and call in some favors. She wanted me to quit, so she made sure it happened. What other explanation was there?

I haven't had a drink in more than eleven years and haven't wanted one. Whatever demon I had has fled for good. If I can stop drinking, anyone can. I'm reminded of an old joke:

> How many psychiatrists does it take to change a lightbulb?
> One, but the lightbulb has to want to change.

CHAPTER 10

The Dead of Winter

Death is only dreadful for those who live in
dread and fear of it. Death is grace, the greatest
gift of grace that God gives to people who
believe in him. Death is mild, death is sweet and
gentle; it beckons to us with heavenly power,
if only we realize that it is the gateway to our
homeland, the tabernacle of joy, the everlasting
kingdom of peace.
—Dietrich Bonhoeffer

I remember my grandmother Nan lamenting the deaths of her friends and saying, "There's hardly anyone left," and I couldn't relate. At the time, everyone I loved was still with me, and I hadn't suffered any losses. Since then, almost everyone in my family older than I has gone: my grandparents, Mom, Dad, my aunts and uncles, and even a husband ten years younger than I was. The only exception is Mom's baby brother, my uncle Jerry, who is doing well in his eighties. Many bright lights in my life have gone out, and I miss them. As long as she was alive, Mom missed them too and always remembered them in her letters.

Pop will be dead 20 years in May. My gosh! Nanny,
who was always the sick one, outlived them all.

I try to convince myself that I'm not afraid of death, and I don't
live in fear of it. But I do worry about those close to me dying. I
know how I react when a loved one dies: I cry and make myself
sick. I cry especially when I'm driving alone in the car and at
night when it's time to sleep. I am never quite the same afterward.
When someone close to me dies, I eventually tell myself I have
two choices: go on or not go on. If I choose to go on, I make the
most of it. If I chose not to go on, I am done.

This chapter is about dealing with the deaths in my family. At
age seventy-five, it's a good time to reflect on my experiences—
not that I feel death is imminent. Reflecting on it helps me to
appreciate life.

My grandparents started dying in the mid-1960s. The
first bereavement I remember devastated Mom. Her father, my
grandfather Pop, died in the spring of 1964 of heart failure. I
was nineteen years old and in college. I had a final exam two
days before his funeral. There were no makeup tests; you either
took the exam or had to retake the course. I upset my mother
by staying behind to take the test while she went to Kingston. I
missed the wake, but I made it to the funeral in time.

Pop's dead body was the first one I saw up close. I thought his
dead body was strange but not scary. When I touched his skin, I
found that it didn't feel like living skin anymore. Whatever had
made Pop a person was gone. Where had he gone? Was his soul
in heaven? Mom dreamed of him and missed her father dearly:

> I feel in a blue mood today. I had a dream about
> Pop last night & we were dancing. When the
> music stopped & I went to break away, he held me
> & didn't seem to want to let go. It's still so vivid
> in my mind. I can't seem to forget it.

It was a few years before death struck again, and again, it hit Mom the hardest. On a cold, wintry day in December, Mom got a phone call that Nan was in the hospital with heart problems. I received the news at home in Ohio. None of us were too worried since it didn't seem like a crisis.

The next day, Jerry called and said Nan was alive, but her heart had stopped working. Mom dropped everything to take a bus to New York. I considered making the trip, but it was snowing, and I had two small children to look after. By now, I worried about Nan and cried by myself. The weather was bad in upstate New York, and Mom's bus ride took almost twelve hours. At the station, Jerry met her with the news that Nan had died. Mom didn't get to say goodbye to her beloved mother.

Nan was buried next to Pop with her prayer book, under a headstone that didn't reveal her age. (Our Nan was proud!) Mom always wrote about the anniversary of her mother's death:

> Nan will be dead 10 yrs on Dec. 21. I remember that day so well, that horrible bus ride to Kingston in snow & sleet. We've all had masses for her.

> This is the day Nan died in 1973. It still hurts when I think about it. I think of so many ways I could have done more for her.

> Today is Nan's birthday. I think she would have been 89, it's hard to believe. I got up & went to 8 o'clock mass. I sure didn't feel like it, but I felt she would appreciate it and she would do it for me.

Watching my mother deal with her mother's death was painful, but I never thought about losing my own mother. I thought she was invincible.

As adults, my mother and father were healthy. Mom had

migraines, which ran in the family, but nothing else bothered her until she got older. Then she had arthritis in her knee and a broken bone or two from falling. She downplayed her problems, complaining only that they interfered with her housecleaning. She hated to sit still. She was always doing something—cooking, cleaning, washing, weeding. Even at a young age, I couldn't keep up with her. She was an active and energetic person. Mom often mentioned cleaning in her letters:

> I started cleaning your father's room. What a job, it's wall to wall books. I just did the windows & some woodwork. It will take me all summer to do a good job.

Mom was an extraordinary housecleaner. She cleaned the way a houseful of servants would have done. For spring cleaning a bedroom, she would strip the bed and flip the mattress, vacuum the mattress and box springs, dust the bed and all furniture, wash the woodwork and floorboards, take the light fixture off the wall and wash it, take all screens out of the windows and wash them, clean the windows and sills, wash the curtains and floor, and clean the closet—all that for a twelve-foot square room. It tires me just to list her chores. She died in June 2009, but her spring cleaning for that year had been done, a little at a time and in pain.

Mom and Dad used to wonder who would die first. Dad had been active as a fisherman for much of his life, but that changed when he retired in his fifties. In retirement, he stocked up on vitamins and supplements and sat in his recliner. He consulted his medical books, which sometimes caused him to be concerned about his health, but he never acted on his worries.

> Your father discovered a small lump on his wrist & now he's worried about that. He thinks it might

be a blood clot. His problem is he doesn't have
enough to do, he sits here by himself all day with
his books & TV.

Mom was a devotee of walking. She walked every day,
regardless of the weather. At the age of seventy-four, she was
walking at least two miles a day and also using the stationary
bike. Once, she met an old geezer—her term—while out walking
who said she must love to walk. She replied cheerily, "I'd rather
be home sitting in a chair, reading the paper." She didn't walk for
her enjoyment; she walked for her health, and she was fanatical
about it. She knew she had to be fanatical; otherwise, it would be
too easy to miss one day and then another and finally succumb to
the lures of the easy chair. As a plus, the walks were a quiet time
for her to say the rosary.

She walked almost every day, until one day she got light-
headed and blacked out. She fell face-first into the middle of a
street. A kind couple found her and called an ambulance. At
first, they thought her crumpled body was a dog that had been
hit by a car. The ambulance took her to the hospital, where she
was banged up enough to be admitted. She was fitted with a
pacemaker, which took care of her light-headedness and, most
importantly, kept her alive.

After a few days, she felt better and wanted to go home, but
the hospital wouldn't discharge her unless she had someone at
home to help her. Reluctantly, she called me and asked me to
help out. I dropped everything, scheduled time off from work,
booked a flight, and rented a car. I was there within twenty-four
hours. Later, she apologized for inconveniencing me. It was no
inconvenience. I would have done anything for my mother and
was glad to help, because she asked for so little.

After that, she gave up walking and started to lose her energy
and robustness. She wrote regarding her fall,

Today I met the girl who helped me the day I
fell. Her husband was the one who called 911.
I thanked her for taking the time to help me
because she was on her way to work.

The first death I faced intimately was my father's. As head of
the house, he went first to show his family how to die. As ever, he
was the stoic and brave Norwegian, distant son of warrior kings.

After Dad retired from fishing and a life on the Atlantic Ocean,
he stopped smoking and drinking, but he lived a sedentary
lifestyle. Dad loved nothing more than to read a book or doodle
all day. Mom often wrote about his inactivity.

I think he should get out more, he just sits here
& thinks about everything & reads his medical
books. I'm going on a trip to the Hilltop Steak
House. I can't sit home all the time with your
father or I'll get like him.

Dad had respiratory problems for years from smoking heavily
when he was younger. He often had trouble breathing and coughed
a lot. Mom wrote about his health from time to time but never
said she was worried.

Your father is coughing quite a bit today. He's
taking some kind of pills & he thinks if he can
cough enough, he'll feel better.

I last spoke to Dad on the phone some time over the Christmas
holidays in 1996, just a few weeks before he died. He wasn't
feeling well; he was coughing and having trouble breathing. Since
he had emphysema, the respiratory problems weren't unexpected,
but my sister and I still worried about him. His calves ached. A
few years earlier, Dad had been hospitalized for blood clots in his

legs. He hated the hospital and liked doctors only a little better. The clots went undiagnosed for a while because Dad said the doctor never asked if he had pain in his legs. Apparently, Dad expected doctors to ask questions until they landed on the right one. He was a stubborn man. He finally went to the doctor for the breathing problems, but I don't know if he ever mentioned the leg pain. My sister and I pleaded with him to please tell the doctor all his symptoms, but we don't know if he did. The doctor took a chest x-ray.

On New Year's Eve, Dad went to bed around eleven o'clock, not bothering to see the New Year in. I think he knew he was dying. A few days earlier, while reading his medical book, he'd told my mother, "Well, I guess this is it." When Dad didn't come down for breakfast the next morning, Mom checked on him in his bedroom, my old room. He was dead, already cold. There were no final goodbyes, and there was no time to tell Dad we loved him. It was a new year, and he was gone.

We think Dad died from a pulmonary embolism because of his history with blood clots, but it could have been a heart attack. His death certificate says only that his death was sudden. If he didn't mention his leg pain to the doctor, he died of sheer pigheaded stubbornness. But he died a good death, pain free in his own bed. He didn't go down with his ship during a horrific storm in the middle of the ocean. He didn't drown. He just fell asleep. My father, Knut Knutsen Vikre, descended from the early Viking kings of Norway, died overnight while I was sleeping six hundred miles away. When I went to sleep, he was alive; when I woke up, he was gone, and I hadn't felt a thing.

On New Year's Day, Mom called early in the morning. My husband, Scott, answered the phone, turned to me, and said, "Your father's dead." I snatched the phone from his hands and frantically asked Mom what had happened. She told me he'd died in his sleep and not to worry about her. I wanted to be with my mother, but she said not to visit; there would be no service for

Dad, and the weather wasn't fit for travel. She told me to wait until the spring, when we could have a good visit. In the face of death, Mom looked toward the spring.

I cried nonstop for the next two days. I cried at home and at work. Then, when crying was making me sick, I stopped. The crying burrowed deep into my heart, where it still remains.

The doctor had taken a chest x-ray of Dad about a week before his death. He called after the holiday to tell my mother that Dad was fine. Mom said, "No, he's not. He's dead." Mom never pulled any punches.

Dad had donated his body to the Boston University Medical Center. After he died, an ambulance came and took his body away, and he was gone. When the ambulance arrived to take Dad's body, the driver, upon seeing all his vitamins and supplements, said, "How did this guy ever die?" Mom said he would've been furious to know she outlived him.

He was buried in Tewksbury, Massachusetts, under a small headstone provided by the Department of Veterans Affairs. Neither Mom nor I ever visited his grave. We both had a fear of driving around Boston after that terrible trip with my father years ago. Our fear kept us home. Was that unkind? He was gone, and we knew that nothing we did would bring him back. Instead, we prayed for his soul. My sister and her husband visited his grave. Mom wrote,

> On the way back from Maine, Geraldine & Richard passed the town of Tewksbury so they stopped to find the cemetery where your father is buried. They found it without any trouble. Geraldine was the one who found your father's grave. He is buried in a cemetery associated with the Boston University Medical Center.

Mom and Dad had both chosen to donate their bodies to science. Cremation was part of the contract with the medical center. My sister and I agree that we wish Mom had a grave to visit. Graves are places to connect with the dead. They are part of nature. Although I think of Mom often, I find it hard to connect with her ashes on a shelf in my den, nestled among many books. For this reason, I want to be buried in the earth with a modest headstone telling the world who I was.

After Dad died, Mom didn't talk about him much. She grieved for him in silence and said she was fine. But she lost a worrisome amount of weight, and she seemed depressed, although she wouldn't own up to it. The following excerpts are from letters she sent shortly after Dad died:

> I'm still finding it a little hard to adjust. It's strange to be here alone, but time will help.

> I'm doing a good job on the tea you sent for Christmas. I also ate one of the candy bars. I wish your father could have had one of them.

> I haven't been having that jittery feeling too much.

> I'm giving a scholarship in your father's memory to Old Rochester Regional High School.

> Some days I have that heavy feeling & then other days when I'm busy I don't have it.

> Every day I wake up with such anxiety but it goes away during the day, thank heavens.

Over time, and with a prescription for depression, she resumed her usual activities. But for the rest of her life, there was a sadness about her that I hadn't noticed before. A light had gone out in her. Maybe their marriage hadn't been as bad as I'd thought.

Mom told me that in her dreams, Dad was always smiling. I like to think that wherever he is, Dad is happy. I hope he found the afterlife he didn't believe in. I think of Dad whenever I'm near the ocean. I think of his hard life on the sea and the loneliness he must have felt. He always came home to us, and now the sea brings him home to me.

After Dad died, I asked my mother if she wanted to move in with me. I had plenty of room for her, and we would have had each other's company, but she didn't want to leave Geraldine and her family or her home and her friends. Likewise, I didn't want to move in with Mom and leave my daughters and their young families. They needed me.

I hated living away from my mother, especially since she too was living alone. I sent her books I knew she'd like and called her often. Her letters kept a hearty tone, which was reassuring, and I knew my sister called her every morning.

By the summer of 2000, I was grieving for my husband, Scott, and for my aunt Tillie. My husband had died in the past October, my favorite cat had died in February, and Aunt Tillie had died in June of that year. There were so many deaths. But I still had Mom.

I first became concerned about Mom's health when she lost consciousness on one of her beloved day trips; she was in her late seventies, and she wrote,

> Yesterday on our day trip, after we ate in New Hampshire, I started feeling queasy. I asked Ellen (girl with one-tooth) to go outside with me. I'm glad she did because I passed out. I don't remember falling, I just remember coming to & wondering why I was on the ground. After I got up & walked to the bus. When I sat down, I passed out again but I don't remember doing it. This morning my doctor couldn't find anything

wrong except my blood pressure was a little high. He thought it would be a good idea to have the arteries in my neck checked with ultra sound. Sorry to burden you with my problems but I know you would want to know.

She didn't go on many trips after she had that fainting spell. Mom was getting old. When she was nearing her eighty-fifth birthday, my daughter Lisa did something special for her: she organized an email campaign for birthday cards. The goal was to have Mom receive eighty-five cards for her eighty-fifth birthday. Both of my daughters sent the email to a wide distribution list, which we later found out got passed along many times. Mom got more than three hundred cards. If the senders didn't know Mom, they sent comments about my daughters. They told her what a pleasure it was to know them. It was a happy birthday for Mom, perhaps one of her last happy ones before she began her long goodbye. The cards, like the letters, were treasured, saved, and passed along when Mom died. Geraldine has them in a box along with other things that were Mom's.

Mom stayed active and had a quick mind almost to the end. During one of my last visits to her house, she wanted to garden but felt too weak to do any digging. She had gotten a few new plants, as she did every spring. I planted them for her. I should have done more. She also asked me to vacuum her basement, which was always spotless. Rather than doing it with grace, I made fun of her old vacuum, telling her what an antique it was. She said with good spirit, "Everything in this house is old, Kath." Then, to prove my importance, I told her I had found a cobweb. She almost went into a panic, as I had known she would. What evil had crept into my tongue? I'm sorry for my insensitivity, Mom. I was teasing you, and I didn't know you were dying.

Toward the end, she was diagnosed with stage-four cancer and had surgery. For two and a half years, she was treated with various types of chemotherapy, which had insidious side effects. During that time, she lived alone and kept her complaints to herself. She was hospitalized after a neighbor found her unconscious from an ulcer and dehydration, both caused by the chemo. From the hospital, she was transferred to a nursing home, and she told the ambulance driver to get her there before *Dancing with the Stars* came on.

Mom went into the nursing home two months before she died. For the first six weeks, she was interested in her surroundings. Geraldine would put her in a wheelchair and take her to pray the rosary in the chapel; she also took her to Mass until Mom was too sick to attend. As sick as she was, Mom worried about not going to Mass, although the priest had assured her she didn't have to go. Geraldine and Mom were in awe of an old lady with dementia who sat in the front row of the chapel and knew all the responses in the Mass by heart.

My sister took Mom on outings around the hospital. Mom liked seeing the residents. Geraldine said they had a good laugh when *Wheel of Fortune* came on TV. As they walked the hallways, the theme song blared from every room.

Geraldine visited Mom almost every day. I had planned to visit, but I didn't make it in time. I didn't know she was dying that fast.

Mom always said she didn't want to end up being a burden to anyone. She never was.

> If I get to the point where I can't care for myself,
> put me out of my misery.

I last spoke to her by phone about a week before she died, when she rallied enough energy to talk to me and to her brother Jerry. My sister helped her make the two phone calls from the nursing home. We spoke only briefly. My last words to her were "I love you, Mom."

"Love you too, hon," she said as if we had been saying it all our lives. I had a flashback to my babyhood—lots of motherly hugs and a memory of Mom calling me hon many times long years ago. I remembered her love. She died peacefully on June 20, at the start of summer. Dorothy Catherine Hotaling, my mother, my touchstone, had slipped the surly bonds of earth.

Unfortunately, poor Geraldine had gone home for supper, so she wasn't with Mom when she died. But for the last two weeks of her life, Mom slept most of the time. I'm sure Geraldine was in her heart. Mom lived a good life and died with dignity. Her faith carried her off to eternity. Of all the deaths I experienced, Mom's death was the hardest on me. Thank God she went before me. I don't know if she could have handled my death or Geraldine's. I barely handled hers, but I had relative youth and good health on my side. On the other hand, Mom had her strong faith in God.

My mother had given life to me and raised me. She was a trusted friend and teacher. When she died, it had been two years since I retired. My house seemed lonelier than ever. I missed her voice, her advice, and her comfort. I wanted to call her. When I came across her letters in my linen closet, it was as if she had come back to me, as any mother would to comfort a grieving child. In death, as in life, she was there for me.

So many deaths. My grandparents. Dad. My husband. Mom. Aunt Tillie. Uncle Billy. My beloved cats. I didn't want to be like Queen Victoria and mourn for the rest of my life. Underneath all my anxiety and depression was a happy—well, happier—person wanting to get out. If only I could figure out how to get out of my misery and quit feeling sorry for myself.

CHAPTER 11

After Winter Cometh the Spring

> The secret of change is to focus all of your
> energy, not on fighting the old, but on
> building the new.
>
> —Socrates

Six months after I was born, the atomic bombs of war decimated people and cities in Japan. I knew nothing about it. I was a baby, wrapped in blankets, cuddled, fed, and protected by my mother and provided for by my seafaring father. I was at peace. I knew nothing of the world going on outside the safety of my mother's arms. Occasionally, in her letters, Mom filled me in on my early life.

> I remember I was wheeling you in your carriage
> on Hanratty St. when Franklin Roosevelt died. You
> were a month old. Franklin was only 63 when he
> died & I thought he was an old man at the time.

Despite the devastation, Japan is still the Land of the Rising Sun. The sun still shines over Mount Fuji, and the cherries still blossom. The country rebuilt itself, and its culture survived, proving that we humans are pretty resilient. Signs of birth, death, and rebirth are everywhere. All we have to do is look.

My mother lived a good life and wasn't afraid to die. Her faith carried her through her struggles, and in the end, it took her home. We survive our struggles, become stronger, and carry on. Spring inevitably follows winter.

As Wordsworth said, "The world is too much with us." I was born content and enjoyed a happy childhood, but somewhere along the way, the world encroached on my contentedness and became too much with me. I went from cuddly and content to unhappy, anxious, and depressed. At times, my life was rude and rudderless, and I made mistakes. I wasn't always kind, I drank a lot, and I took some bad risks and made bad choices. I lost track of my spirituality, my faith. Yet I survived. I even flourished. How did this happen? As I think back, I realize I had these in my favor: my family's love, my mother's religion, and my knowing I could do better.

Although I haven't always realized it, faith was the foundation upon which I lived my life. It gave me a belief system and taught me that goodness matters and that prayers are heard. I chose to have faith and accepted my lot.

As I lived, I learned, and Mom was my faithful guide. She guided me over her lifetime, and when she was gone, she guided me again from her letters. I read her letters and became reacquainted with love and loss, hope and despair, life and death. Over time, I found a way out of the darkness and into the light, leaving anxiety and depression behind. I am a different person now than when I started writing this memoir. I am unconquerable. As William Ernest Henley writes in "Invictus,"

> I am the master of my fate,
> I am the captain of my soul.

Like many people, I didn't follow a straight path through life. I floated through my early years of education, high school, and college. Once I started making choices, I made bad ones. I married twice and didn't find mad, crazy love. But I found valuable lessons. I watched a young husband die in my arms. I felt his soul leave his body.

My parents never let me go, no matter what I might have done to hurt them. They always forgave my mistakes. The most life-changing mistake of my life—getting pregnant—turned into my greatest achievement. As painful as it was and despite how it hurt my mother, I chose life. I got married and had a baby. That choice led to another baby, seven grandchildren, and who knows how many descendants. It led to my taking a wonderful job that sustained me for more than thirty years and made me feel good about myself. The job gave me a good pension, which allows me to see the world and help others who are in need. How blessed my life has been because of a mistake.

Mom's love for me lives on in my love for my daughters and my grandchildren, the next generation. Already, at young ages, they are facing life's challenges. The world they know caught up to mine and raced beyond it. They live in a world complicated by changes in culture, fewer civilities, more political strife, and relentless technology. They are stalked by killer viruses.

I know a way out of hell.

—Ghandi

Take heart! From my experiences, I found that life is good, just, and worth living. I am determined to enjoy life and live it to its fullest. In my midseventies, I'm the most content I've been since childhood. I found that my spirit, which has been there all along, is pure and noble. I am brave. I am a wise woman. Along with knowledge, I have heart. Most importantly, I have a superpower that is available to everyone: grace. It is a blessing given to everyone who accepts it. I am blessed.

Over my lifetime, I found ways to deal with those struggles that robbed me of my well-being. I prayed, read self-help books, took seminars, got counseling, listened to my mother, and did lots of reflection and analysis. Not everything stuck, but some things did. I keep them in my bag of tricks for when I need a little help. I call this bag of tricks "Seven Steps to a Better Life."

Seven Steps to a Better Life

1. Love Thyself

Since I was taught as a child not to be selfish, I had a hard time getting a grasp on the concept of self-love. Over time, I learned what self-love is. Self-love is believing I am worthy of love, having values and beliefs I cherish, being at peace with who I am, and not being dependent on others for my happiness.

When I was at my lowest point of self-esteem after my divorce, I didn't know who I was. I was a reflection of my husband. If you asked for my opinion, I would give my husband's opinion. My favorite color was also his. My favorite food? His.

Gradually, I took stock of who I was and what I believed in— what *I* believed in. I found that I am a unique person with solid beliefs, core competencies, and inherent goodness. I value myself and don't allow others to treat me badly. This is self-love. I face life from a position of strength. I give to others. I don't take from them.

What Mom Said

Did I tell you I was supposed to go on a trip to NY with the girls from work? I'm not going, the trip was booked up. I've decided to buy myself some gold chains as a consolation. Of course I'm not telling your father. All he thinks about is putting money in the bank. I don't know what he's thinking, because when he wants something he gets it. He says he doesn't want to be the richest man in the cemetery. But if I should want some gold, then I'm spending too much.

Yesterday they were playing some jitter-bug music from World War II & I wondered if I could still do it. By gosh! Bad knee & all, I jitter-bugged all around the kitchen floor & was pretty proud of myself. Today is the first day in a long time that I can bend my knee going down the stairs.

2. Give Thyself a Break

Accidents happen. Sometimes I hurt people without meaning to. Sometimes I do silly things and embarrass myself. When I'm not happy with myself or something I've done, I put the unpleasantness behind me and start with a fresh slate. I get a good night's sleep and wake up refreshed and ready to tackle a new day. Mom wasn't perfect, but she never stopped trying to improve. She looked forward, not back. As Ragnar Lothbrok said on the TV show *Vikings*, "Don't waste your time looking back. You're not going that way."

I try not to be too hard on myself for mistakes I have made or pain I've caused. I'm human; I'm fallible. Mom forgave me many times. I can forgive myself. I give myself a break and move on.

What Mom Said

Leanne was crying when she got to the restaurant. She went to CVS to get Mother's Day cards & she hit a woman. I thought she hit the woman while the woman was in her car, but Leanne was backing out & the woman walked in back of her. Last night Leanne called & said the woman was going to be O.K. She had a broken elbow & a gash on her leg that would need plastic surgery. The police told Leanne it wasn't her fault. Leanne was feeling better last night. She said all she could think of was she might have killed someone's mother on Mother's Day.

Geraldine calls me every night. When I didn't hear from her on Mon. I got to feeling sorry for myself. I'm saying no one cares, here I am, all alone & I don't ask for much, just a phone call. Turns out the phone was dead & she had been trying to call me all night.

3. Choose Goodness

When I have a difficult decision to make, no matter how big or how small it is, I consider the options and choose the one that results in the most goodness, or the most love, or the least stress. I avoid stress as much as possible. It lowers your immune system, and bad things start to happen.

For the most part, I choose life over death. But sometimes a compassionate death is called for. I believe that everyone, and every living thing, deserves the right to a quality life and a good death.

When my old cats were dying and were struggling to survive, I decided it would be merciful to end their suffering. I promised each cat that I would be with him or her until the very end. I stayed with them and never cried in front of them, so they didn't get upset. I kept my promises.

When I look back on my life, I find that many situations that started out looking bad ended up being good. I could even call them blessings instead of curses. For example, my father was often insensitive to my mother. But he lived a hard life on the sea to provide for her, and he was loyal for more than fifty years. Many would call him noble. Despite his rough demeanor, my father was a good man, and he did the right thing.

What Mom Said

It's been very hot. I asked the mailman if he would like a cold drink & he ended up having lunch here. Your father had made a huge vat of fish chowder.

A neighbor told me she went grocery shopping and when she pulled in the parking lot, she saw a cart with a bag of groceries & she took it home. Over $100 worth of food. Some poor soul probably went back for it hoping an honest person found it. I told her she should have taken it into the store, but she said the clerks would have kept it. I wish she hadn't told me.

4. Be Forgiving

Learn to forgive. Mom forgave me for slacking off in school and for getting pregnant. She forgave her family their every indiscretion or misdeed. I learned that it's pointless to hold a grudge or past hurt or even to regret. Holding on to grudges, hurts, and regrets benefits no one; you tend not to learn or grow. You stay in place. I believe we should forgive people who have hurt us, not necessarily for their sakes but for our own. Forgiveness gives us a more peaceful state of mind and less stress.

I forgave Mom and Dad for being unemotional. What did emotions matter, when they loved me, protected me, gave me opportunities, and gave me a little sister? With all my heart, I love my parents.

I did have a hard time forgiving my second husband for spending our savings on a young lady and dying without telling me why he did that. I felt betrayed and hurt. But I hadn't taken a good look at myself. I had been negligent. For more than twenty years, Scott had done our bookkeeping. He did all our banking and paid our bills. He paid our taxes. I took no interest or responsibility in our finances. I enabled his infidelity by my aloofness. If I had behaved differently, maybe I could have nipped the whole problem in the bud. Also, and possibly most importantly, he was dealing with a stage-four cancer. I don't know what his fears cost him or what might have alleviated his sufferings. Maybe the young lady helped him by being a diversion. If that was the case, how could I begrudge her?

I decided I was making the issue bigger than it needed to be. Overall, the marriage was good for more than twenty years; we had fun, and we didn't argue. He genuinely cared for the kids. I lost money, but I also lost my memories of the good times. In writing this book and remembering, I forgave him.

What Mom Said

> Geraldine was talking to Leanne's former guidance counselor & she was telling her she uses Leanne as an example to everyone because Leanne never let her school work suffer when she was going through her teenage problems.

5. Find the Lights

We all need lights in the darkness to show us the way. Some of my mom's lights were her faith in God and her Catholic religion. They taught her the rules, told her how to live, showed her the way to salvation, and, finally, guided her to her death. Like her mother before her, she never wavered from her love of God and her belief in Catholicism. No matter the pain or inconvenience, she attended Mass at least once a week until she was close to death. To her, there was no excuse to miss Mass, not the weather, old age, or poor health. She prayed every day, at least an hour every morning.

Her other lights were people she could count on. Her sister, Tillie, was her closest friend. They were kindred spirits. They believed in the same things and loved the same people. They were soul mates. She loved her other siblings, Billy and Jerry, as well and always her mom and dad.

I learned to find the people on earth who shine light upon me. They open my mind and expand my thinking. When I am around them, I feel good about myself and become a better person. When I find the lights, I keep them close and make sure they stay lit. I don't want to be in the darkness. My sister is once again my best friend. She keeps me bright and engaged. My daughters and their children are my special lights. They connect my past with my future.

What Mom Said

Mother Theresa is coming here Wed. Some nuns from her order are living in a convent across from St. Lawrence Church. I think she's as close to a saint as I'll ever see.

6. Do What's Right

> If it is not right, do not do it, if it is not true,
> do not say it.
> —Marcus Aurelius

Mom tried to do what was right. She was a good mother to my sister and me. She tended to our daily needs and showed us the world through outings and travel. I never heard her say a harsh word or speak back to her mother or father. She respected them, and she loved them for who they were—the parents who gave her life. I always wanted to tell my mother I loved her; it was the right thing to do. I managed to tell her that when she was on her deathbed. I never told my dad I loved him. I regret that. I tell him every day in my heart and hope he hears.

Do the right thing at the right time, regardless of how hard it is.

What Mom Said

I got to church by myself yesterday in the snow without any problems. I was proud of myself. The worst part was trying to park around the church because the priest doesn't have the sidewalk plowed.

I got to thinking I never tell you I love you & I do.

Today is Nan's birthday. I think she would have been 89, it's hard to believe. I got up & went to 8 o'clock mass. I sure didn't feel like it, but I felt she would appreciate it and she would do it for me.

It's finally election day. I guess I'll vote for Ron. I feel sorry for Mondale, I think he's very honest, but I don't think he would make a strong president. I can't vote for George Bush tho. Nanny is going to vote for Mondale because he's Norwegian.

7. Love, Love, Love

Mom's letters taught me the importance of all kinds of love. Her love shines through her words. I'm touched by her love of her family and her kindness to her neighbors and coworkers. She loved tending her garden and feeding the wild animals that visited her. She was loving to Dad in many ways. She cooked his meals and cleaned his room.

I strive to experience love to its fullest, and like Mom, I love people, animals, and nature. To the best of my abilities, I surround myself with people who care for me, and I always keep a door open to help a stranger. One summer day, I gave a juicy apple to a young man from Dubai who was sitting on my lawn while waiting a long time for a bus. "To quench your thirst," I said. Months later, right before he returned to Dubai, he knocked on my door and gave me a box of chocolates. I've given money to animal rescue groups, fundraisers, and friends in need. I've even supported a few movies—we all need a little Hollywood. I expect nothing in return.

What Mom Said

Your father & I feel so bad about your cat Bitsy. I'm sorry now I wasn't a little more tolerant with her but she could be a pest. I still feel bad 'tho.

I shed a few tears over Whitey. She was my favorite of your cats.

I watched the Tony's [sic] last night. One fellow that won kissed his boyfriend & then in his speech he said, "I thank my lover, my husband."

On Sundays the girls at work bring in treats. Your father objects every time I bring something. He said those girls were too fat (look who's talking). One week I bought a bag of chips to bring in & he carried on so, I left them home for him.

I'm having a real good time reading about Richard Burton. He was a very interesting person. As far as I'm concerned, I think meeting Elizabeth Taylor was his downfall. In some ways she was good for him, but all in all, I think he would have been better off without her. Those children didn't't have much of a life, they had everything but love & attention.

So there you have my seven steps to a better life. It wasn't until I finished writing this section that I started thinking about all the religious, mystical, and historical meanings of the number seven. There are seven gifts of the Holy Spirit and seven Wonders of the Ancient World. It was a coincidence that I found seven steps for living a happy, fulfilled life. Not that this finding makes my words better or more profound. It simply lets me know that maybe I am in the ballpark.

CHAPTER 12

The Circle of Life

> When we die, our bodies become the grass, and
> the antelopes eat the grass. And so we are all
> connected in the great Circle of Life.
> —Parental advice from *The Lion King*

The Triskele Tattoo

Recently, I forced myself to overcome a paralyzing fear of flying and traveled to California to meet a friend I had not yet met. It was an enormous undertaking for me. No one in my family thought I would have the nerve to do it. I took a big risk, but the adventure turned out to be rewarding.

Flying over America and then over the mountains into California, I felt I was flying to a magic kingdom. I had known the mystique of Hollywood for years, as my mom had, and there I was, flying into LAX on a wing and a prayer.

My first sense of California was the heat. It was warm and embracing like a hug, not stifling like the humid heat of the Midwest. Next, I noticed the palm trees. In all my years on this planet, I had never seen one. They are tall and majestic, reaching toward the stars. And there was the beach. The sand was white and pristine, unlike Atlantic beaches, which have rocks and seaweed. I waded into the Pacific Ocean, a sea my father hadn't known. I looked up from the sea and saw mountains. This truly was a magical land. Looking to the mountains, I was awed by their beauty. I was reminded of my trip to the American West, where I had been awed by mesas, canyons, and buttes. Now I was taken by warmth, sand, mountains, and palm trees. This was another world to me, and I embraced it.

On the beach at Santa Monica, I felt energized, younger, and renewed. My friend showed me the sights around Los Angeles. We talked into the night over hot cups of tea, palm trees, and surf. Mom loved Hollywood, but she never visited it. Who would have thought I'd be the adventurous one?

In Los Angeles, I got my first tattoo. I wanted something meaningful. It would be emblazoned on my skin for a lifetime. It finally came to me. I chose a triskele, an ancient Celtic symbol consisting of three interlocked spirals. It symbolizes how we live, die, and are reborn throughout our lives.

The tattoo parlor, located in West Hollywood, had eclectic steampunk decor and was well lit and clean. I took a few photos of the decor, thinking to incorporate some of it at home. I observed one young lady getting her entire torso tattooed with a snake. Her skin was perfect. It was without blemish and porcelain white. The snake was dark blue and gracefully wrapped around her from front to back. It was beautiful, and for the first time, I saw tattooing as an art form.

My tattoo artist was kind and wanted to make sure I was prepared for any pain. Getting tattooed was surprisingly painless. When it was done, I felt brave and confident. I chose different colors for the three spirals to represent the birthstones of my daughters and me. I love my triskele tattoo. It's usually within my line of sight, and it reminds me of my life, death, and rebirth.

Life, Death, and Rebirth

As children, we know all we need to know about the world. Put simply, for many of us, our world is our mother. She feeds us, dresses us, tells us stories, and puts us to bed. As we grow up, we learn about things from other people—fathers, priests, teachers, friends, coworkers. Our world becomes bigger and more frightful. We learn about death. But if we are lucky, we also learn that death is not the end; it is a stop on the circle of life. We are immortal.

We are an Easter people and alleluia is our song.
—Saint Augustine, fourth century

I am an Easter person. I choose to believe in life after death. There is nothing unnatural in death. It is standard fare. I have no idea what follows death, but I believe it is life of some kind. So I choose not to fear dying. For me, this is a leap of faith as big as a swan dive into deep water.

I ask myself, as I once asked my father, Do I believe in heaven, a state in which all souls live in eternal happiness with God? I believe in the possibility of it and that our time on earth matters. I believe we are reborn after we die, maybe even more than once. Whether this rebirth involves heaven, another life, or something else, no one knows. I trust in God, an eternal Creator and Nurturer, to take care of things for me. I don't fear the future.

The wonderful thing about the idea of being reborn is that it can happen many times during life. We don't have to wait until we die. I was reborn into a new way of living after I became a widow, after I retired, after Mom's death, and again after I stopped drinking. I was reborn when I overcame my fear of flying, took a long plane flight, and stood in the Pacific Ocean.

Being a widow meant not having to report to anyone, a husband or a boss, only to myself and my beliefs. This was significantly less stressful. For the first time in decades, I was free to make my own choices.

Retirement was the death of my working world. It meant a new way of living, one unconnected to schedules and clocks and in which I didn't measure my value on the success of my work. It meant the loss of many acquaintances. The challenge was to keep my mind busy. I found genealogy, a challenging and fulfilling hobby, and traced my ancestry to the old Viking kings of Norway and the early Dutch settlers of New York City. As I grew older, I had time for personal reflection. I also found time to travel. In retirement, I was reborn with freedom, new interests, less stress, and more time for myself.

Mom's death broke my heart. For the first time in my life, I had to make my way without her. When Mom was alive, I always knew she was looking out for me. I never thought about dying alone, because we talked on the phone every day. Mom and I, both widows, looked after each other. When she died, I felt alone. I was depressed. But I chose to go on without her. I chose life. Mom's letters reminded me I was capable and competent. I could do this. And I found that Mom was still with me in spirit. She had joined my guardian angel in protecting me.

A few years ago, I changed my last name back to the name I was born with, my father's name. There was pride in that name. I had embraced my Norwegian roots through my ancestry discoveries, and I remembered and loved my father. It was the name I identified with. It was the name I wanted to leave the world with. I chose who I was and told the world.

Becoming Me: One

The summer Mom died, I quit drinking. It was a bad habit I had for more than thirty years. I hadn't planned to stop. I just decided that drinking had outlived its usefulness to me. I believe that some higher power might have been at work. I quit with no problems and no looking back. It felt good to be sober all the time. I released myself from a prison I had entered.

I took stock of myself. It was time to say goodbye to anxiety and depression and get to know myself. I took advantage of any tool I could find. I talked often to my sister and a few trusted friends, got counseling at a behavioral health clinic, and took a wellness program. I downsized my belongings. I got rid of anything I didn't need.

I wrote this book. Writing was good for my soul.

I found Mom's spirit and my own. I cleaned my house so that when the time comes to leave this gentle earth, I'm ready, and my bags are packed.

Becoming Me: Two

There's a happy ending to the story I told about the baby who was adopted. When Leanne was fifteen, she said goodbye to her baby boy, whom she gave up for adoption. She thought she might never know what became of him. One day Leanne got a call. It was the baby, grown up now and married, with children of his own. When I heard the news, I couldn't believe the adopted baby had been found. My sister and I were joyous. A miracle had graced our lives.

Mom died before knowing Baby John Doe would be found. I hope the news reached her in heaven. Or did she pull heavenly strings to make this possible?

Leanne chose life. She gave birth to a baby and gave him up so he could have a good life. In the end, it all worked out. What was lost was found. It was the circle of life. Our family was reborn, and we were together.

> Everything will be okay in the end. If it's not
> okay, it's not the end.
> —John Lennon

Becoming Me: Three

The letters, having served their purpose, are safely back in a box. I can open them anytime. They renewed my spirit when it desperately needed renewing. They helped me reach my mother and keep her words alive. In spite of life's struggles, I am still here, and I am better than ever. I am happy, my mind is active, and I have good health, both physical and emotional. In spite of getting older, I know I still have contributions to make and relationships to tend.

It will come as no surprise to readers of this book that I loved my mother. I missed her after she died, grieved for her for many years, and was depressed. Then I found the letters she'd sent me over the decades. In the letters, I found the spirit of my mother and renewed my own.

Now my memories are strong, and she walks with me. She continues to guide my moral compass. I often consider how Mom would have handled a situation I'm faced with, and then I do what she would have done.

She put on a brave front when she was troubled or in pain. She was horrified at the thought of becoming a burden to anyone. She never was. Although she didn't graduate from high school, she had an active and open mind and tried to improve it. She read constantly. She learned new words. She wrote letters. She ate moderately and exercised by walking miles almost every day for as long as she was physically able. She cared about politics and always voted. She was one of the Greatest Generation: stoic, hardworking, and loyal. She was my mother.

In addition to being a reader, I am now a writer like my mom. I am at peace with the world. With this sense of peace, I decided to write one last letter to my mother.

Dear Mom,

I can't believe you've been gone more than ten years. In fact, I still can't believe you're gone at all. Every day I want to talk to you, and after all this time, I can still use your advice. I miss you. I wonder if you were lonely after Dad died. I wish I had visited you more often.

I was heartbroken after you died. I found your letters and unearthed your spirit, which guided me to a better place. You were always a good mother, and no mother wants to see her child unhappy. You came back to me through your letters. Your wisdom and sense of humor shook me out of the doldrums and brought me happiness.

All through my life, you were like a pixie sprinkling your magical dust on me so that I could fly. You enabled me to do better than I thought I could. You always encouraged me to strive for excellence, and this paid great dividends in college and at my job. Thanks for always seeing the best in me.

In reflecting on your letters, I understand that we all struggle, die, and are reborn. I have no doubt you are in heaven. I wonder if Dad is in heaven with you. You had unshakable faith in God, and you've already performed some miracles; you helped me to stop my drinking, and you reunited Leanne with her adopted baby.

The last years of my life are laid out before me. At the moment, I am happy to have the house to myself and my family near. I have nature, animals, fresh air, comfort, and a good outlook.

I'll be content until I pass away and join you. What a day that will be!

I'm writing a book about our lives, based on the letters you sent me. I cry every time I pick up a few to read; writing this book has been hard on me but rewarding. I want to write it for you—for us. Thank you for being such a good mother. You couldn't have been better.

I miss you. I love you.

Love,
Kathy

I am a mother, the gentlest and most fierce creature God ever created. Mothers will do anything for their children. They love them unconditionally and will fight to the death for their protection. This is the way it is. I am now my mother in the great circle of life. Without thinking, I emulate her love for family and kindness to others. I talk to people I don't know. I wish them well. I spread joy.

There is one more thing I must do before closing this book and putting away my mother's letters. I must write a letter to my children.

Dear Lisa and Tracey,

I'm living a full and happy life; I'm content. You are a big part of my happiness. I expect to continue to enjoy life and be active into my nineties if the fates allow. I have some traveling to do and more stories to tell. Don't count me out. And don't be sad when I die. Death is inevitable, and I'm ready for it. I can leave any time with no regrets. Since seeing Scott die, I'm not frightened by death, although I am a little anxious. But his transition from life to death was so peaceful. I don't live in fear of it.

I've always lived my life as an example to you. I didn't want to lecture you, so I showed you what patience, gentleness, and forgiveness were like. You, in turn, showed me your unique traits and talents. Lisa's patience and Tracey's artistry are just two examples. We are different, but we've always been together. I remember talking to you when your dad and I split up. I said we were in it together, the three of us. You never let me down.

You're both so mature and level-headed that I have little advice for you. I'll give you just a few helpful tips. Take deep breaths, and drink lots of water. These are good for your health. And avoid stress as much as possible. When I decided to do this, the first thing I did was to throw out the bathroom scale. Not that I advocate a poor diet and obesity. If you minimize stress, you'll be happier and more at peace with yourself and the world, and you'll have better immune systems.

By all means, choose happiness at every turn. It's okay to be happy even in the face of tragedy. Even happy people mourn. Finally, take time to appreciate what you have, your beautiful selves and partners, your children, and this beautiful world. I love you to the moon and back!

Love,
Mom

CPSIA information can be obtained
at www.ICGtesting.com
Printed in the USA
BVHW031027111020
590782BV00001B/54

9 781982 254520